checkp■int

Endorsed by
**University of Cambridge
International Examinations**

english

3

Sue Hackman   Alan Howe
Revised by Sue Bonnett

**⑤ HODDER
EDUCATION**

PART OF HACHETTE LIVRE UK

ACKNOWLEDGEMENTS

The Publishers would like to thank the following for permission to reproduce copyright material:

Photo credits
Cover © Randy Faris/Corbis; **p.3** Carla Sachar, Bloomsbury Publishing plc; **pp.12–13, 14, 16** © 2002 by Walden Media, LLC. Photographs reproduced by permission of Walden Media. Walden Media is a registered trademark, and the Walden Media skipping stone logo is a trademark of Walden Media, LLC. All rights reserved. For more information about Walden Media's educational productions, please go to www.walden.com; **p.28** *all* © Hodder Education; **p.31** *tl* © Getty Images, *tr* © J T Turner, Getty Images, *bl* © Bob Battersby/BDI Images, *br* © Ed Horn, Getty Images; **p.32** © Hodder Education; **pp.67, 69–71** © Donald Cooper/Photostage; **pp.110, 114, 123, 128, 129, 130, 131, 132** © The Dickens House Museum.

Text credits
pp.1–3, 4–5 Louis Sachar's website www.louissachar.com; **pp.6–8, 10, 18–19** Excerpts from *Holes* by Louis Sachar. Copyright © 1998 by Louis Sachar. Reprinted by permission of Farrar, Straus and Giroux, LLC.; **pp.79–80** *Of Mice and Men* by John Steinbeck, Penguin Books, 2004; **p.125** *Flour Babies* © Anne Fine, 1992, Hamish Hamilton. Reproduced by permission of Penguin Books Ltd; **p.138** *How Not to Raise the Perfect Child* by Libby Purves, Coronet Books, 1999.

l = left, *r* = right, *t* = top, *b* = bottom

Every effort has been made to trace all copyright holders, but if any have been inadvertently overlooked the Publishers will be pleased to make the necessary arrangements at the first opportunity.

Although every effort has been made to ensure that website addresses are correct at time of going to press, Hodder Murray cannot be held responsible for the content of any website mentioned in this book. It is sometimes possible to find a relocated web page by typing in the address of the home page for a website in the URL window of your browser.mM

Orders: please contact Bookpoint Ltd, 130 Milton Park, Abingdon, Oxon OX14 4SB. Telephone: (44) 01235 827720. Fax: (44) 01235 400454. Lines are open from 9.00 to 6.00, Monday to Saturday, with a 24-hour message answering service. Visit our website at www.hoddereducation.co.uk.

© Sue Hackman, Alan Howe, Sue Bonnett, 2005
First published in 2002 as *New Hodder English Gold 3*
This title first published in 2005 by Hodder Murray,
an imprint of Hodder Education, part of Hachette Livre UK
338 Euston Road
London NW1 3BH

Impression number   10 9 8 7 6 5 4
Year   2010 2009 2008 2007

Typeset in 13 on 20pt New Century Schoolbook by Fakenham Photosetting Limited, Fakenham, Norfolk
Illustrations by Kate Sardella of Ian Foulis & Associates, Peter Bull Art Studio
Cover design by John Townson/Creation
Printed in Malaysia

A catalogue record for this title is available from the British Library

ISBN-13: 978 0340 887 394

CONTENTS

INTRODUCTION

Welcome to *Checkpoint English*, which comprises three fully revised editions adapted from books in the *Hodder English Gold* series. *Checkpoint English 1* introduces pupils to a wide and challenging variety of English experiences and assignments, which are then progressively built on and broadened in *Checkpoint English 2* and *3*. However, teachers may wish to use these books to supplement their own schemes of work, or other materials.

Raising standards and covering curriculum requirements

We have taken as our prime directive the advancement of pupil learning. All the materials in *Checkpoint English* offer the very best of current practice. We know that pupils in the early levels of literacy need explicit instruction and scaffolded activities. We have provided both in the context of purposeful work and quality texts. Each book contains one unit of work that addresses basic skills as a focus of work in its own right and consolidation activities have been built in later. The units are therefore very suitable to address the Reading, Writing, Usage, and Speaking and Listening objectives of the CIE Checkpoint English Curriculum.

Checkpoint English addresses the appropriate number of set texts and includes many more. Pre-twentieth-century literature is amply represented in both fiction and non-fiction. You will find here a catholic range of genres, tones and forms, but we have resisted simplified versions in favour of abridgement. Although speaking and listening is not tested at this level, the Checkpoint curriculum maintains its importance in language development is such that it should play a major part in the curriculum alongside reading and writing. Therefore, we have made particular efforts to ensure that speaking and listening is fully represented in the series, not merely as incidental group talk but as a purposeful activity in its own right.

Structure

Checkpoint English consists of three books and a CD. Each book is divided into units, which have been arranged across the three years to establish, revisit and consolidate key skills.

Although the units have been placed in an order which offers pupils a varied and progressive experience of English, you can use the book in a flexible way, linking units with others or with texts you want to teach.

Whilst we have introduced basic skills directly through key units, we also assume that teachers will continue to support individual pupils by giving them feedback on their oral and written performance, and that spelling, punctuation and grammar will be part of this continuing work. The Usage sections for each unit have activities with a more focused attention on sentence structure, grammar, punctuation and spelling, and vocabulary. Unit Four in this book gives advice and activities for preparing for the Checkpoint English tests.

Progression

Checkpoint English 1, 2, and *3* form an incremental programme of work with clear goals written with the expressed intention of raising standards in English. The course offers far more than a sequence of self-contained lessons or starting points because progression is built into each unit, between each book and across the course as a whole. Key elements of English are focused on once in each year, and incidentally as a part of other units.

Assessment

Assessment is an integral part of each unit. However, checklists, recording sheets and assessment grids are deliberately not included, as it is most likely that you have already developed a workable system. Teaching by units enables you to collect evidence of pupils' achievements periodically, and systematically, at the end of each unit. The book provides the pupils with focused tasks and explicit criteria for evaluating how well they are doing, and what they need to improve on.

Activities

The initial material and activities of each unit are designed to introduce pupils to the focus for the sequence of work, and to engage their interest. There is then a series of tasks designed to help pupils to develop specific areas of knowledge, understanding and skill. Several pages are given to consolidating new knowledge or skills in context.

Using *Checkpoint English*

Many of the units are free-standing and teachers will find them sufficiently flexible to introduce extra material or to extend their use beyond a half-term. Texts have been chosen for their quality and for their richness in classroom study, as well as for their accessibility, and relevance for the age group. Where it has been impractical to reproduce whole texts, we have produced extracts to support the close study of key passages.

In addition, the CD provides support where it is most helpful. To promote reading skills, we recommend that pupils conduct close study activities using the text as well as the CD so that they can learn how to find particular words, phrases and information in the text. Where the CD icon appears (shown on the right) the text which is being studied is provided on the CD as well.

For your convenience, a number of pages have been designed as *photocopiable*. These pages contain activities that pupils will do best if they are involved in hands-on work.

CHECKPOINT ENGLISH CURRICULUM OBJECTIVES

Introduction

The teaching of English should develop pupils' abilities to use language effectively, to communicate in speech and in writing and to respond with understanding and insight to a wide range of texts. Whilst speaking and listening is not tested at this level, its importance in language development is such that it should play a major part in the curriculum alongside reading and writing. An integrated curriculum is envisaged in which speaking and listening activities commonly support learning.

Reading

Pupils should:

- Read a wide range of narrative, non-fiction and media texts. These may include novels, short stories, drama scripts, poetry, journals, diaries, letters, leaflets, magazines, newspapers and advertising matter
- Recognise explicit meaning, select, collate and summarise facts and ideas, using their own words where appropriate to demonstrate understanding
- Recognise and comment on opinions expressed by a writer
- Understand vocabulary and comment on a writer's use of language, such as the use of an informal or a formal style, or the choice of words to create an atmosphere or to persuade the reader
- Recognise implied meaning, such as the inference of character from what someone says or does in a text, or the meaning contained in an image
- Comment on the main features of narrative writing, such as character, setting, theme, and the way in which a plot is put together
- Demonstrate understanding of features of narrative, non-fiction and media texts by developing them in their own discussion and writing, for example, a further episode about a family portrayed in a book, or providing the wording for an advertisement

Writing

Pupils should:

- Write for a variety of purposes, such as to inform, explain, describe, explore, imagine, entertain, argue, persuade, instruct, analyse, review and comment
- Write in a wide range of forms, such as stories, poems, playscripts, autobiographies, personal letters, diaries, formal letters, persuasive writing, advertising copy, newspaper reports and articles, reviews, arguments, information sheets, notes and leaflets
- Begin to develop a sense of audience and to engage the reader's attention
- Structure their writing, using paragraphs and sequencing events, details and ideas within paragraphs
- Use varying styles of writing appropriate to different forms

Usage

Pupils should:

- Use full stops, capital letters, commas and question marks to make meaning clear, and show awareness of other forms of punctuation, including the presentation of dialogue
- Spell correctly most of the words they use
- Learn a range of vocabulary appropriate to their needs, and use vocabulary in speech and in writing to clarify meaning and to interest their audience
- Use a range of increasingly complex sentence structures to communicate meaning and to give fluency to their speech and writing
- Use correct grammar, including tense, case and word order

Speaking and listening

Pupils should:

- Speak for a variety of purposes, such as to explain, describe, narrate, explore, analyse, imagine, discuss, argue and persuade
- Participate in speaking and listening activities in order to discuss and prepare assignments
- Begin to make significant contributions to group discussions and help to plan and to give group presentations
- Hold conversations with others on familiar subjects
- Develop the ability to listen courteously to others and to be sensitive to turn-taking
- Practise speaking fluently at an appropriate pace
- Practise speaking clearly at an appropriate volume
- Use a range of vocabulary and sentence structure to make speech interesting and convincing

TEACHER GUIDANCE

UNIT ONE: HOLES

READING	WRITING	SPEAKING & LISTENING
Interpretations of text	Exploratory writing	Standard English
Author's standpoint	Influence audience	Group organisation
Prose text	Counter-argument	Drama techniques
	Impartial guidance	Convey characters and atmosphere

TEACHING SEQUENCE

The suggested sequence anticipates that you will use this unit as the basis for a 'staged' reading of the whole novel with the class, using the materials provided in the unit for focused discussions and activities that will gradually build up and deepen pupils' responses as they go along.

Week 1:	Introduction to author; key themes in the novel. Begin novel; first impressions, reading log
Week 2:	Continue reading novel to Chapter 32; characters and relationships
Week 3:	Read to Chapter 43; plot and narrative techniques (links with characters from the past)
Week 4:	Read to end of novel; ending and overview
Week 5:	Writing to argue and advise

TEACHERS' NOTES

In this popular novel, Louis Sachar explores the experiences and interaction between young characters in a juvenile detention centre. The novel will provide pupils with an accessible text that is also challenging both in its content and in its use of narrative devices. As the teaching sequence above illustrates, we suggest planning to teach the novel in a series of weekly lessons focusing on key sections and teaching objectives, using the materials in the unit as stopping-off points. Pupils are asked to keep a reading log as they progress through the novel, as a way of catching their ideas and developing a written response to key episodes. This works best if you can develop a dialogue with pupils in their reading log, prompting reflection by asking questions and recording, briefly, your own ideas and responses. Extend and enhance the unit by gathering a collection of Louis Sachar novels.

UNIT TWO: NEWSROOM

READING	WRITING	SPEAKING & LISTENING
Synthesise information	Presentational devices	Standard English
Readers and texts	Integrate information	Interview techniques
Author's standpoint	Effective presentation of information	Compare points of view
	Influence audience	Analyse bias
	Balanced analysis	Group organisation

TEACHING SEQUENCE

Lessons 1–2:	A story breaks
Lessons 3–4:	Putting a story together (Later that day, Headlines, Picture power and Layout)
Lessons 5–7:	Writing and presenting the news (Presenting the news, Unscrambling the news)
Lessons 8–12:	Hijack story

TEACHERS' NOTES

You can build a topical and interesting unit by collecting interesting newspaper covers and television bulletins in the weeks prior to teaching this unit.

Lessons 1–2: Note that you will need a number of newspapers for one of the activities. Organise pupils into groups with at least one copy per pupil. You could reproduce this activity using yesterday's stories from the short early evening TV news, and ask pupils to put them in order before showing the outcome.

Lessons 3–4: Good starters for these lessons would include wall displays of recent front pages with pictures or headlines blocked out with plain paper. Pupils could speculate about what would appear in these blanks before you show the originals. Collect front pages which feature striking images.

Lessons 5–7: You will need a video camera and a quiet setting for recording the news.

Lessons 8–12: Aim to cover a bulletin each lesson, as if in real time. You will need the video camera each lesson, but rotate the recording of the lesson's bulletin among the groups.

UNIT THREE: MACBETH

READING	WRITING	SPEAKING & LISTENING
Analyse scenes	Balanced analysis	Evaluate own drama skills
Major writers	Cite textual evidence	Drama techniques
		Compare interpretations
		Critical evaluation

TEACHING SEQUENCE

Lesson 1:	Introduction to themes: role play
Lesson 2:	Opening scene
Lessons 3–5:	Act 1; the art of persuasion
Lessons 6–8:	Act 2; investigating the murder
Lessons 9–11:	Act 3; staging the banquet scene
Lessons 12–13:	Act 4
Lessons 14–15:	Act 5
Lessons 16–17:	Each group focuses on a different character
Lesson 18:	Group presentations
Lessons 19–20:	Writing about the play

TEACHERS' NOTES

The unit supports an exploration of the play over a period of approximately half a term. You will need a class set of *Macbeth* so that you can treat the play as a script to be interpreted and explored through a range of drama, role-play and reading activities. Each act in the unit is summarised through using a cartoon version, but we recommend that you support pupils' learning by using a video of the play and the BBC *Animated Tales* version as well. Use video to introduce a scene, or to accelerate from one closely studied scene to the next. A number of the drama activities will benefit from working in a flexible space. The unit concludes with a series of 'Focus on . . .' study pages which invite pupils to review their understanding of the play by considering key characters; an active way of using these will be to subdivide the class into groups, each of which works on one character, culminating in oral presentations.

UNIT FOUR: PREPARING FOR THE CHECKPOINT TESTS

READING	WRITING	SPEAKING & LISTENING
Information retrieval	Review own writing	
Note-making at speed	Planning formats	
Evaluate own critical writing	Formal essay	
	Creativity in non-literary texts	
	'Infotainment'	
	Explain connections	
	Cite textual evidence	

TEACHING SEQUENCE

Lesson 1:	Introduction
Lessons 2–3:	Tackling reading questions – Non-fiction reading (Paper 1)
Lesson 4:	Fiction reading (Paper 2)
Lessons 5–6:	Planning non-narrative writing (Paper 1)
Lessons 7–8:	Planning narrative writing (Paper 2)

TEACHERS' NOTES

This unit contains a lot of good advice, but pupils may pass over it. A good approach is to ask pupils in advance what might be in the bullet lists of advice before you read them together, and at the end of the unit, you can ask them to reconstruct the lists from memory.

To extend this unit:

- Show examples of real questions on real papers and allow pupils time to plan answers in small groups.
- Allow time to answer questions as a whole class, so you can model how to marshal materials and how to express and structure answers.
- Allow pupils to practise individual answers, then share ideas, examples and comments in a whole-class debriefing.
- Share mark schemes.
- Run a mini-moderation based on anonymous past pupil efforts.

The objectives in bold are key objectives that are fully developed in the unit.

UNIT FIVE: SCANDAL

READING	WRITING	SPEAKING & LISTENING
Note-making at speed	Exploratory writing	Evaluate own talk
Compare texts	Influence audience	Evaluate own listening skills
Readers and texts		Compare points of view
Author's standpoint		Analyse bias
		Identify underlying issues
		Evaluate own contributions
		Consider viewpoint
		Group organisation

TEACHING SEQUENCE

Lessons 1–3:	Exploring the issues
Lessons 4–5:	Facts and opinions
Lessons 6–7:	Dilemmas
Lessons 8–9:	Review of speaking and listening

TEACHERS' NOTES

You could develop this unit by:
- comparing treatments of similar stories in different newspapers
- following the development of a major story.

UNIT SIX: WHAT THE DICKENS!

READING	WRITING	SPEAKING & LISTENING
Authorial perspective	Narrative techniques	
Compare writers from different times	Descriptive detail	
Author's standpoint	Cite textual evidence	
Rhetorical devices		
Major writers		

TEACHING SEQUENCE

Lesson 1:	Dickens' London
Lesson 2:	Dickens captures the reader's attention
Lesson 3:	Pen portraits
Lesson 4:	Naming names
Lessons 5–6:	Dickens paints a picture
Lesson 7:	Goosebumps
Lessons 8–9:	Oliver Twist: So what's new?
Lesson 10:	A grisly end
Lessons 11–12:	Dickens' life and times

TEACHERS' NOTES

This unit features a number of favourite extracts from Dickens' work. You may well have televised versions available to show the class.

Lesson 1: It would be useful to have slides or illustrations to show.

Lesson 3: Share the pen portraits produced, pointing out effective techniques and praising good efforts.

Lessons 5–6: Demonstrate how to search and annotate descriptive details on an OHT. This will be useful in the tests.

UNIT ONE

Holes

A book will usually give you some information about the author. Doing a little extra research on the author sometimes helps you to enjoy and understand a book.

Louis Sachar is the author of *Holes*. Read this extract from his website.

I was born in East Meadow, New York in 1954. My father's office was on the 78th floor of the Empire State Building, which I still think is pretty cool, even if those were simpler times than today. When I was nine years old, we moved to Tustin in Orange County, California, a rural area just beginning to suburbanize. At that time, there were orange groves all around, and the local kids would often divide up into teams and have orange fights. The 'ammo' hung from the trees. My experience from Little League was good training as an orange warrior. I can only assume that we weren't very popular with the grove owners.

I enjoyed school and was a good student, but it wasn't until high school that I really became a devoted reader. One of my favorite authors was E.B. White.

After high school, I attended Antioch College in Ohio. It wasn't long, though, before I received word of my father's sudden and unexpected death. I returned to California to be near my mother and took a semester [term] off from school. During that time, I had a short but surprisingly successful career as a Fuller Brush man. For those of you too young to know what that is, I went door-to-door selling household goods, especially brushes, mostly to housewives.

Before long, I returned to college, this time to the University of California at Berkeley. I was an economics major, but I also loved Russian literature. I soon got it into my head that I should learn Russian so that I could read my favorite Russian classics in their original language. I started taking Russian classes, but after about a year, I realized that the only language I was ever going to be reasonably competent in was English. I soon dropped my Russian class and began searching for something to take its place.

On campus one day, I saw the unlikely sight of an elementary school girl handing out flyers. I took one from her. It said—'Help. We need teachers' aides at our school. Earn three units of credit.' I thought it over and decided it was a pretty good deal. College credits, no homework, no term papers, no tests, easier than learning Russian, and all I had to do was watch over a bunch of kids at Hillside Elementary School. I should mention that before this I'd had no particular interest in kids.

So, I became a Noontime Supervisor, or 'Louis the Yard Teacher' as I was known to the kids. It became my favorite college class, and a life changing experience. I found that I didn't like any of the little stories that the children were reading, and as I had always wanted to write, I decided to try my hand at a children's book of my own. Hillside Elementary became the inspiration for my first manuscript, *Sideways Stories from Wayside School*. All the kids in the book are named after kids I knew at Hillside. I even included myself as a character known, not surprisingly, as 'Louis the Yard Teacher'. In the meantime, I graduated in 1976 with a degree in economics.

My first job after college was in a sweater warehouse in Norwalk, Connecticut. Not the best use of my economics degree, perhaps, but it did allow me time to write. After about a year, I was fired (my enthusiasm for sweaters was insufficient), and I decided to go to law school. *Sideways Stories from Wayside School* was accepted for publication during my first week at Hastings College of the Law in San Francisco. This was certainly good news, but it created a long internal struggle as I tried to decide whether to be a lawyer or an author.

In 1980, I earned my degree and then went on to take the bar exam. I recall staying up all night with a group of friends, waiting to see if we had passed the exam (which was required to practice law). Happily, I passed, but I quickly realized that I wasn't as thrilled as I should have been. By now, it was clear that writing was my first career choice. Still, I needed a job, so after some procrastination [thinking], I began practicing law to finance my writing habit. *Johnny's in the Basement* and *Someday Angeline* followed *Sideways Stories*.

It wasn't until 1989 that my books began selling well enough that I was finally able to stop practicing law and devote myself fully to writing.

Louis Sachar

Activity

Read the information on pages 1–3 from Louis Sachar's website. He has included personal information at the same time as promoting his book.

- What information would you include on your own website?
- Do you have a particular interest you could talk about?
- What personal information could you use to promote this interest?

Why I wrote the novel

Where did you get the idea for *Holes*?

No, I didn't live next door to a juvenile correction facility [a prison camp for teenage criminals]. Actually, I never start with a full idea of what I'm going to write. I usually just start with a piece of a character and then see what develops. In this case, I didn't start with a character; I started writing about Camp Green Lake and it developed from there. I suppose the initial inspiration for writing about the camp came from the heat of summers in Texas. At the time I began the book, we had just returned from the relative coolness of a vacation in Maine to the Texas summer. Anybody who has ever tried to do yard work in Texas in July can easily imagine Hell to be a place where you are required to dig a hole five feet deep and five feet across day after day under the brutal Texas sun.

How long did it take you to write *Holes*?

A year and a half. A book like *Marvin Redpost: Is He a Girl?* is simply written and relatively short, taking four to six months to finish. In contrast, *Holes* took a year and a half to complete. I went through five rewrites before sending it to my editor. It occurs to me now that Stanley was sentenced to Camp Green Lake for eighteen months, which was exactly how long it took me to write *Holes*. I arbitrarily [randomly] chose the length of his sentence early on. Maybe on some unconscious level, I knew how long it would take.

Did you find the characters taking on a life of their own as you were writing?

It happens every once in a while when you're writing that certain characters seem to leap off the page and take over the book, and that's what happened with the story of Kate and Sam. I had expected to make Kissin' Kate a complete villain, but when I started writing about her I ended up making her someone else entirely; it surprised me.

Why do you think the book's lead character, Stanley Yelnats, connects with so many children?

Stanley isn't a hero-type. He's a kind of pathetic kid who feels like he has no friends, feels like his life is cursed. And I think everyone can identify with that in one way or another. And then there's the fact that here he is, a kid who isn't a hero, but he lifts himself up and becomes one. I think readers can imagine themselves rising with Stanley.

What was the hardest part of writing *Holes*?

People often ask me how I managed to tie everything together at the end, but that wasn't the hard part. I knew how everything was going to fit together. The hard part was laying out the strands throughout the story, telling the story of Kate Barlow and of Elya Yelnats and Elya's son, without it getting in the way of Stanley's story.

The other problem I had occurred when Stanley was digging his hole for the first time. I wanted the reader to feel what a long, miserable experience this is, digging those 5' by 5' holes. But how many times can you say, 'He dug his shovel back into the dirt and lifted out another shovelful'? My solution was to interweave two stories, bringing more variety to the tale. Stanley's anxious first days at Camp Green Lake are set off against the story of his ancestor, Elya Yelnats, whose broken promise to a Gypsy results indirectly in young Stanley's bad luck.

***Holes* is sweet and charming, but it is also darker and scarier than your other books. The warden, for example, mixes rattlesnake venom in her fingernail polish and threatens to scratch Stanley. Was it your intention to write a frightening tale?**

My daughter, Sherre, who was in fourth grade [aged 9] when *Holes* came out, surprised me when she told me that the warden was scary. I had never really thought of the warden as scary or that the scene was especially disturbing. Rattlesnake venom, well, it's almost cartoonish. It's like a situation from that campy old TV show, *Batman*. It was never my intention to write a grim story, and I don't think it is. For instance, I came up with the idea of the boys digging holes because I liked the irony, not because it was harsh. While they were … digging to build character, the camp warden actually had hidden and dishonorable reasons for demanding this chore. I wanted *Holes* to be fun and adventurous.

Activity

- Read the information from the website. Discuss in groups what you expect this novel to be about.

- What events might happen in it? Take your ideas from what the author says about himself and the background to the story.

- Imagine that you are planning a story based on a young girl or boy who spends some time in a juvenile detention centre (a prison camp for teenage criminals). What ideas would you have for the **plot** (what happens in the story)?

Green Lake

The setting of Green Lake plays an important part in the plot of *Holes*.
Read the opening of the novel.

There is no lake at Camp Green Lake. There once was a very large lake here, the largest lake in Texas. That was over a hundred years ago. Now it is just a dry, flat wasteland.

There used to be a town of Green Lake as well. The town shriveled and dried up along with the lake, and the people who lived there.

During the summer the daytime temperature hovers around ninety-five degrees in the shade – if you can find any shade. There's not much shade in a big dry lake.

The only trees are two old oaks on the eastern edge of the 'lake'. A hammock is stretched between the two trees, and a log cabin stands behind that.

The campers are forbidden to lie in the hammock. It belongs to the Warden. The Warden owns the shade.

Out on the lake, rattlesnakes and scorpions find shade under rocks and in the holes dug by the campers.

Here's a good rule to remember about rattlesnakes and scorpions: If you don't bother them, they won't bother you.

Usually.

Being bitten by a scorpion or even a rattlesnake is not the worst thing that can happen to you. You won't die.

Usually.

Sometimes a camper will try to be bitten by a scorpion, or even a small rattlesnake. Then he will get to spend a day or two recovering in his tent, instead of having to dig a hole out on the lake.

But you don't want to be bitten by a yellow-spotted lizard. That's the worst thing that can happen to you. You will die a slow and painful death.

Always.

Now read this extract from Chapter 23.

One hundred and ten years ago, Green Lake was the largest lake in Texas. It was full of clear cool water, and it sparkled like a giant emerald in the sun. It was especially beautiful in the spring, when the peach trees, which lined the shore, bloomed with pink and rose-colored blossoms.

There was always a town picnic on the Fourth of July. They'd play games, dance, sing, and swim in the lake to keep cool. Prizes were awarded for the best peach pie and peach jam.

A special prize was given every year to Miss Katherine Barlow for her fabulous spiced peaches. No one else even tried to make spiced peaches, because they knew none could be as delicious as hers.

Every summer Miss Katherine would pick bushels of peaches and preserve them in jars with cinnamon, cloves, nutmeg, and other spices which she kept secret. The jarred peaches would last all winter. They probably would have lasted a lot longer than that, but they were always eaten by the end of winter.

It was said that Green Lake was 'heaven on earth' and that Miss Katherine's spiced peaches were 'food for the angels'.

Katherine Barlow was the town's only schoolteacher. She taught in an old one-room schoolhouse.

Activity

- Compare Green Lake of the past with Green Lake in the present.
- In small groups discuss how the writer uses language to describe the setting of Green Lake.
- How does the writer's description of the setting make you feel about the characters mentioned?
- Write two descriptive paragraphs that could be the opening of a story or the introduction to a character. Make one setting have a threatening atmosphere and one have a peaceful, friendly atmosphere.

Stanley's story

Now read Chapters 2–5 of the novel.

- 'Stanley Yelnats was given a choice. The judge said, "You may go to jail, or you may go to Camp Green Lake."'

- 'He didn't have any friends at home.'

- 'Stanley was not a bad kid. He was innocent of the crime for which he was convicted.'

- 'He smiled. It was a family joke. Whenever anything went wrong, they always blamed Stanley's no-good-dirty-rotten-pig-stealing-great-great-grandfather.'

Activity

- Think carefully about the way the author introduces Stanley. Use the quotations above and what you have read to help you discuss these questions:

  1. What impressions do we get of Stanley's character?

  2. What impressions do we get of Stanley's family?

  3. Why should Stanley not have to make the choice of going to jail or Camp Green Lake?

  4. Why did Stanley make the choice to go to Camp Green Lake?

- Now write some questions of your own. What do you want to find out as you read on?

Starting your own reading log
What is a reading log?

A reading log is a book in which you write down all your thoughts, ideas and questions about the novel you are reading.

PROMPTS FOR WRITING

You can write anything you like in your log, but you might consider:

1. Setting – where and when the story takes place.
2. Characters – the people in the story.
3. Plot – what happens in the story.
4. Language – how the story is written.
5. Themes – ideas and messages you get from the story.
6. Wider reading – how this story compares to others you have read.

You could start your log with the questions you've already thought of, after reading the opening chapters.

This is how one student began her log:

Monday 20/6/2004

'Holes'

I've just started 'Holes'. The setting for the story, Camp Green Lake, sounds very unpleasant and threatening. I don't like the sound of the yellow-spotted lizard. Maybe one of the characters in the story will be bitten by one of them.

I think I am going to like Stanley but I am a little puzzled as to what he may have done in order to have ended up going to Camp Green Lake. I wonder if we will get more details about his great-great-grandfather.

Activity
- Now start your own reading log. Remember you can choose any part of the novel to write about.

Life after Camp Green Lake...

Now look carefully at this section of the novel.

When he got to the tent, he found Mr Pendanski and the other boys sitting in a circle on the ground.

'Welcome, Stanley,' said Mr Pendanski.

'Hey, Caveman. You get your hole dug?' asked Magnet.

He managed to nod.

'You spit in it?' asked Squid.

He nodded again. 'You're right,' he said to X-Ray. 'The second hole's the hardest.'

X-Ray shook his head. 'The third hole's the hardest,' he said.

'Come join our circle,' said Mr Pendanski.

Stanley plopped down between Squid and Magnet. He needed to rest up before taking a shower.

'We've been discussing what we want to do with our lives,' said Mr Pendanski. 'We're not going to be at Camp Green Lake forever. We need to prepare for the day we leave here and join the rest of society.'

'Hey, that's great, Mom!' said Magnet. 'They're going to finally let you out of here?'

The other boys laughed.

'Okay, José,' said Mr Pendanski. 'What do you want to do with your life?'

'I don't know,' said Magnet.

'You need to think about that,' said Mr Pendanski. 'It's important to have goals. Otherwise you're going to end up right back in jail. What do you like to do?'

'You must like something,' said Mr Pendanski.

'I like animals,' said Magnet.

'Good,' said Mr Pendanski. 'Does anyone know of any jobs that involve animals?'

'Veterinarian,' said Armpit.

'That's right,' said Mr Pendanski.

'He could work in a zoo,' said Zigzag.

'He belongs in a zoo,' said Squid, then he and X-Ray laughed.

'How about you, Stanley? Any ideas for José?'

Stanley sighed. 'Animal trainer,' he said. 'Like for the circus, or movies, or something like that.'

'Any of those jobs sound good to you, José?' asked Mr Pendanski.

'Yeah, I like what Caveman said. About training animals for movies. I think it would be fun to train monkeys.'

X-Ray laughed.

'Don't laugh, Rex,' said Mr Pendanski. 'We don't laugh at people's dreams. Someone is going to have to train monkeys for the movies.'

Holes has been made into a film.

Many novels are **dramatised** for the theatre, film, TV or radio.

The extract on page 10 would look very different in script form.

(*Stanley enters tent. The boys and Mr Pendanski are sitting in a circle on the ground.*)

Mr Pendanski: Welcome, Stanley.

Magnet: Hey, Caveman. You get your hole dug?

(*Stanley nods.*)

Squid: You spit in it?

(*Stanley nods again and turns towards X-Ray.*)

Stanley: You're right, the second hole's the hardest.

X-Ray: (*shaking his head*) The third hole's the hardest.

Mr Pendanski: Come join our circle.

(*Stanley sits between Squid and Magnet.*)

> ★ **Glossary**
>
> If you **dramatise** something, you take an existing story and turn it into a play. This happens a lot on TV. Can you think of any examples on TV?

Activity

- Work in a group of five. Each of you take the part of one of the characters:

  Mr Pendanski   Stanley   Magnet   X-Ray   Squid

- Develop the discussion and action between the characters. Think about what the others might want to do when they leave Camp Green Lake.

- Plan and write a script for your play. Perform it live or record it onto a tape as a radio play.

Who's who?

Activity

Can you work out who's who?

- Ask your teacher for a photocopy of these pages, then cut out each picture and paste it in your log.

- Write a short description for each character.

- Study one character in detail and think of questions for all the others.

- As a class, or in a group of four, take it in turns to put each character in the 'hot seat' (see the Help Box opposite). Ask each character questions. Try to find out what kind of person each is:

1. What do they think?

2. What do they want?

3. What are they planning to do?

HELP

Hot-seating

You can hot-seat any of the characters in *Holes*. You will need a volunteer to go into role as the character. The character is then put in the hot seat. The rest of the group asks the character questions. You need to find out as much as you can about the character.

Read on to the end of chapter 28, which ends 'Kate Barlow died laughing'.

Wonderful teacher

Children loved her

Strong willed

Activity

- Draw a diagram like the one above. Write down all of your thoughts about Kate.
- Stick your diagram into your reading log.

Zero's diary

Zero cannot read or write. You are going to help him record his thoughts.

> *Dear Diary,*
>
> *Stanley has agreed to teach me to read and write. I just about remembered the alphabet. I have told him I could learn ten letters a day. I did some figuring out. He seemed surprised that I was good at maths but I told him I wasn't stupid – I just don't like answering questions…*

Activity

Imagine you are Zero. Carry on the diary entry above.

- Think about how you feel.
- Write about the impression that Stanley has made on you.
- Write how you feel about the way the others react to you digging for Stanley. Use some details straight from the novel up to the point when you run off.

HELP

Remember you are writing in the role of Zero – use the same style of language he would use.

Collision course – plotting movements

Read the section of the novel from Chapter 32 to the end of Chapter 43. In this section Stanley sets out to try to find Zero.

Trying to rescue Zero, Stanley crashes Mr Sir's truck

A desperate Stanley carries a very sick Zero up to what they hope is God's Thumb

Activity

- Starting from the moment Stanley crashes the truck, record in your reading log the main events of the journey he takes. Make a note of any links you can see between what happened to characters from the past and the things that Stanley and Zero find on their journey.

- On a photocopy of the map opposite, plot Stanley and Zero's movements in green dots.

- On your photocopy of the map, mark and label, or use an illustration to show any point where a character from the past may have been.

Lizards **and** lies

Read from Chapter 44 to the end of Chapter 47. To focus your attention on the descriptions of the lizards and the lies told in the passages, the text has been coloured in blue and in red. Read the following extract from Chapter 47.

1. 'Why don't you go see if you can take the suitcase from Zero,' the Warden suggested.

   'Yeah, right,' said Mr Sir.

   'The lizards obviously aren't hungry,' said the Warden.

   'Then you go get the suitcase,' said Mr Sir.

2. 'How are you doing?' Stanley asked quietly. He didn't whisper, but his voice was dry and raspy.

   'My legs are numb,' said Zero.

   'I'm going to try to climb out of the hole,' Stanley said.

   As he tried to pull himself up, using just his arms, he felt a claw dig into his ankle. He gently eased himself back down.

3. A little while later he saw Mr Pedanski and two strangers, coming across the lake. One was a tall man in a business suit and cowboy hat. The other was a short woman holding a briefcase. The woman had to take three steps for every two taken by the man. 'Stanley Yelnats?' she called, moving out ahead of the others.

4. The man was more than a head taller than she, and was able to look directly over her as he spoke to the Warden.

   'How long have they been in there?'

   'All night, as you can see by the way we're dressed. They snuck into my cabin while I was asleep, and stole my suitcase. I chased after them, and they ran out here and fell into the lizard's nest. I don't know what they were thinking.'

   'That's not true!' Stanley said.

5. 'It's a miracle they're still alive,' said the tall man.

   'Yes it is,' the Warden agreed, with just a trace of disappointment in her voice.

   'And they better come out of this alive,' Stanley's lawyer warned. 'This wouldn't have happened if you'd released him to me yesterday.'

   'It wouldn't have happened if he wasn't a thief,' said the Warden.

6. 'Why didn't you release him when she came to you yesterday?' the tall man asked.

   'She didn't have proper authorisation,' said the Warden.

   'I had a court order!'

7. Stanley tried to climb out of his hole, using mostly his arms so as not to disturb the lizards too much.

8. 'Thank God!' exclaimed the Warden. She started toward him, then stopped.

   A lizard crawled out of his pocket and down his leg.

9. He steadied himself, then reached down, took hold of Zero's arm, and helped him slowly to his feet. Zero still held the suitcase.

   The lizards, which had been hiding under it, scurried quickly into the hole.

10. The Warden rushed to them. She hugged Zero. 'Thank God, you're alive,' she said, as she tried to take the suitcase from him.

    He jerked it free. 'It belongs to Stanley,' he said.

    'Don't cause any more trouble,' the Warden warned. 'You stole it from my cabin, and you've been caught red-handed.'

11. 'It's got his name on it,' said Zero.

    Stanley's lawyer pushed past the tall man to have a look.

    'See,' Zero showed her. 'Stanley Yelnats.'

12. The Warden stared at it in disbelief. 'That's im…imposs…It's imposs…' She couldn't even say it.

Activity

In a group of six:

- Act out the scene around the hole which contains Stanley, Zero, the suitcase and the lizards. Use the speech that is used in the novel.
- Think carefully about how the characters who appear around the hole react to the boys, the suitcase and the lizards. Use the text in red to help you think about the lies told by the Warden.
- Watch out for the lizards. The text in blue highlights how dangerous they are!

Onions and sneakers – filling in the holes

Read to the end of the novel.

How are onions important to the development of the plot and the ending of the story?

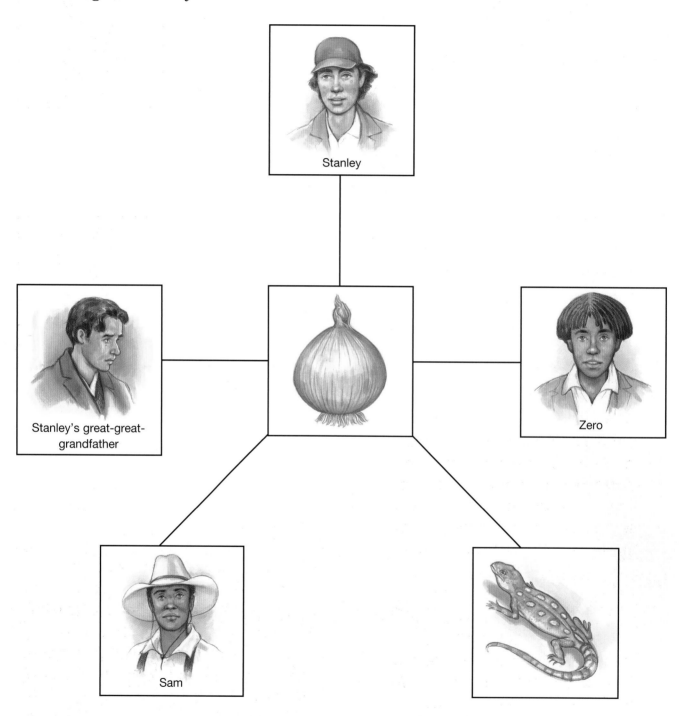

Stanley

Stanley's great-great-grandfather

Zero

Sam

Activity

• Write a short explanation in your reading log.

How are sneakers important to the development of the plot and the ending of the story?

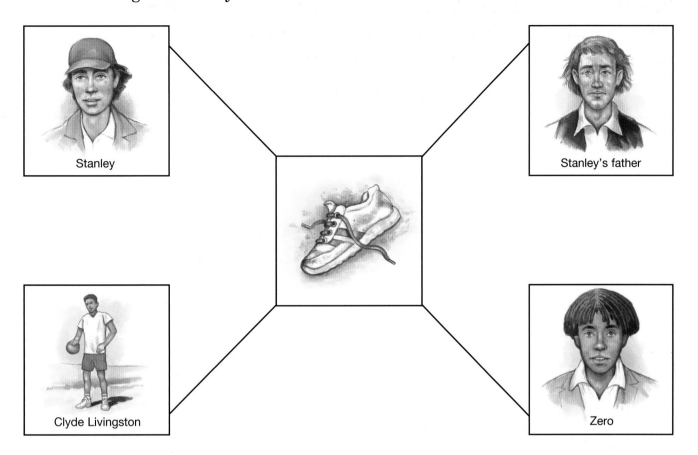

Stanley

Stanley's father

Clyde Livingston

Zero

Activity

- With a partner discuss how the sneaker is connected to the life of each character above. Write the results of your discussion in your reading log using quotes from the novel to justify your statements.

- Onion Sam sold onions. Clyde Livingston takes part in a TV advert for 'Sploosh'. Imagine you work for an advertising agency which has been asked to organise a campaign to promote the sale of onions. Work with a partner to design a leaflet which will convince people of the many advantages of buying and using onions.

HELP

Think about design and format and the different styles of language you could use. You may use descriptive language to make the onion sound beautiful or present information which makes the onion sound important and valuable.

Will you include a recipe to entice people to cook with onions?

Writing to argue

Zero had experienced being homeless. Many people all over the world are homeless and may end up sleeping on the streets.

Read the following letter that was written to the editor of a local paper. It expresses a particular view about homeless people.

Dear Sir

Last night I travelled into town to see a play. It was my wife's birthday and we had been looking forward to the treat for several weeks. The play was very good, but our evening was spoiled when we came out of the theatre to find several people sleeping in shop doorways and another two or three begging for money on the steps of the train station. How can we call ourselves a civilised society if we allow scroungers and layabouts to clutter up our streets? There should be a law banning such behaviour. I would like to see the police take a tough stance and move these people on, and then a pleasant evening's entertainment wouldn't be spoiled by such anti-social behaviour.

Yours sincerely...

Activity

Discuss possible reasons why people may be homeless and living on the streets. Write a reply to the paper. You should aim to present an opposing point of view.

Plan your reply as follows:

- Make a list of the reasons the writer gives for disliking people sleeping rough and begging.
- What does the writer propose as a solution?
- List two or three reasons why this attitude is wrong.
- List three alternative solutions to the problem.

UNIT TWO

Newsroom

Look carefully at this picture of a newsroom.

Information can be beamed to the newsroom via satellite.

Journalists write their articles on laptops.

TV displays pages of news which are updated. This is called Teletext and is like a TV newspaper.

Some stories need to be 'sniffed out' by reporters. Newspapers have reporters around the world.

Some stories can be found on the internet.

Some stories come in on tape.

The editor decides which stories are used and where they go in the paper.

The sub-editor shortens stories to fit the space on the page.

The picture editor decides which picture is best and how to fit it on the page.

A photographer can go with a reporter to take photos of the events.

Activity

- List the different ways that stories can come into the newsroom.
- List the jobs that journalists are doing in the picture.
- Which do you think are the most important jobs?

A story breaks

A lot of news pours into a newsroom. Decisions have to be made –
which news story is important and which is less important?

Reporter Carrie Ferrant is about to watch the late film when she gets a call from her editor.

Carrie is sent to a fire at an old warehouse by the river.

Carrie goes to work finding out all the facts.

Can you tell me what you know?

It started in the basement. It's nearly under control. Five men have been taken to hospital.

She then talks to some witnesses outside the Red Lion pub.

RED LION

We had to leave our house. We live too close to the warehouse.

We smelt the smoke about one o'clock.

Carrie phones in to the newsroom. It is now 3.30am.

Right. I've typed it in. You get home and get some sleep!

Fire swept through the warehouse of Swan and Sons in the early hours of this morning. Twelve fire engines fought the blaze, which could be seen twenty miles away.

In the morning meeting

The Warehouse Fire. Have we got an angle on it?

What is an angle?

An angle is a way of looking at a story. The story of the warehouse fire could be looked at from several angles:

- the bravery of the firefighters

- the loss of precious paintings in the warehouse

- the amazing survival of the church next door

- the possibility that the fire had been started on purpose (arson)

- burning chemicals seeping into a nearby river

- people living near the fire spending the night in a nearby school.

What is your angle?

- If you were Carrie which angle would you choose?
- Which angles do these headlines fit?

FIRE THREATENS ART TREASURES

BRAVE FIREFIGHTERS BEAT WAREHOUSE BLAZE

CITY FIRE: WAS IT DELIBERATE?

- Now write the headlines for the other angles.

But will it make the front page?

Top stories are printed on the front page. Look at the front pages of newspapers.

- What makes a front page story?
- Why are other stories on the inside pages?
- Why do some funny stories appear on the front page?
- Look at different papers. Compare the type of headlines they use.

WHAT ELSE HAVE WE GOT?

WELL, THERE'S A PLANE CRASH IN INDIA – 100 DEAD.

A PLANE CRASH

36hrs

A MAN IN SURREY HAS BROKEN THE RECORD FOR NON-STOP BARKING – 36 HOURS.

THERE'S THE BIG WAREHOUSE FIRE IN LONDON.

BOMB ALERT

A BOMB EXPLODED OUTSIDE BUCKINGHAM PALACE. QUEEN WASN'T HURT, BUT A ROYAL CORGI WAS KILLED.

AND AN OLD LADY FRIGHTENED AWAY A BURGLAR BY TRYING TO KISS HIM.

THE EDITOR MAKES A CLEAR DECISION

NOT THE WAREHOUSE FIRE.

Activity

The editor chooses one serious story and one funny story to go on the front page.

- Which do you think he chooses?

Later that day...

The morning edition of the newspaper has already been printed. But newspapers have later editions, to include news that happens later. Suddenly there is startling news from the warehouse. Part of the warehouse was used as a recording studio. Now three bodies have been found in the smoking ruins. A famous band, The Sub-Zeroes, had been rehearsing in the building. No one has seen them since the fire.

Are the bodies those of the band members?

Reporter Carrie Ferrant looks at her notebook. She talked to witnesses at the fire:

'Just before the fire I could hear music coming from the warehouse.' John Collins, 52, who had been drinking in the Red Lion opposite.

'We had a call at 11.43pm and responded as quickly as we could.' Arthur Morrison, firefighter.

'Thank God the church next door was untouched.' Alice Munro, whose flat overlooked the fire.

'We have no reason to believe anyone has been killed.' Jim Hardy, policeman.

'I did see some scruffy-looking chaps in the pub. They looked a bit familiar, but I don't know much about pop groups! They went out together at about 10pm.' Landlady at the Red Lion.

'I couldn't hear anything from the warehouse at all. No. I can't remember if I was wearing my hearing aid, to be honest with you.' Sid Chesterman, 70, who lives near the warehouse.

Carrie's notes

Carrie made notes about the facts:

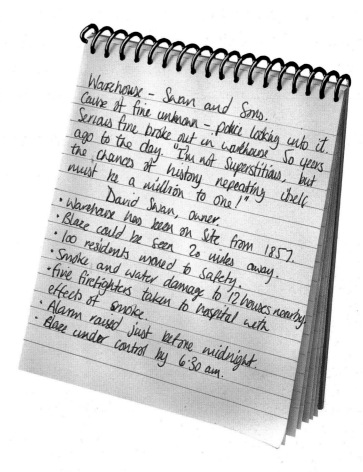

Warehouse – Swan and Sons.
Cause of fire unknown – police looking into it.
Serious fire broke out in warehouse 50 years ago to the day. "I'm not superstitious, but the chances of history repeating itself must be a million to one!"
David Swan, owner.
• Warehouse has been on site from 1857.
• Blaze could be seen 20 miles away.
• 100 residents moved to safety.
• Smoke and water damage to 12 houses nearby.
• Five firefighters taken to hospital with effects of smoke.
• Alarm raised just before midnight.
• Blaze under control by 6:30 am.

Activity

Gathering your story

- Decide on a new angle.
- Read the statements and find information that will fit the angle.
- Read the facts on the pad and find out what is important and what fits the angle.
- Write a headline and three short paragraphs to go in the evening newspaper, using the new angle.

News angle

- Always report the key facts – the story will be new to some readers.

- You can't use everything, so choose information to fit your angle.

- Never lie.

- Pick out the relevant bit by using a highlighter or by underlining.

- Decide the main point of each paragraph.

- Think up links between the paragraphs.

For example: *New information came to light when…*

A new lead has emerged in…

Evidence points to…

Some people think that…

Support for this view was given by…

Witnesses agree that…

Further proof came when…

Headlines

Use one of these headlines for the evening edition, or make up your own.

THREE DEAD IN WAREHOUSE FIRE

MYSTERY DEATHS IN CITY FIRE

ROCK BAND IN FIRE TRAGEDY?

THREE BODIES FOUND IN GUTTED WAREHOUSE

ROCK LEGENDS DEAD?

ARSON ATTACK CLAIMS THREE LIVES

Picture power

A picture is worth a thousand words.

Activity

- Choose the pictures that you think the following papers would use:

  1. A pop magazine
  2. A local paper
  3. A national daily

Layout

Activity

- Look at this page from a newspaper. Match the arrows with the correct terms from the Help Box on page 33.

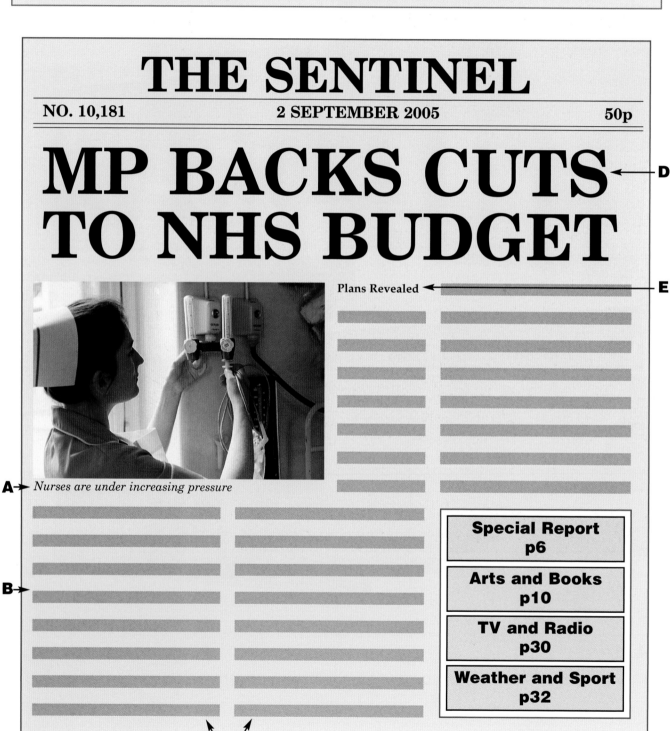

THE SENTINEL

NO. 10,181   2 SEPTEMBER 2005   50p

MP BACKS CUTS ← D
TO NHS BUDGET

Plans Revealed ← E

A → *Nurses are under increasing pressure*

B →

C

Special Report p6

Arts and Books p10

TV and Radio p30

Weather and Sport p32

HELP

Headline:

- The title of the story
- Large type
- Gives the most important fact of the story

Subheading:

- Under the headline
- Gives more information about the story
- Type is smaller than headline

Article:

- The story
- Printed in columns
- Small print

Column:

- Rows of print that run down the page

Caption:

- Line of print under the photograph
- Relates to what is in the photograph

Activity

- Design the front page of your own newspaper to show how the headline, pictures and story would appear.

Presenting the news

Could you be a newscaster? The job of a newscaster is:

- To introduce stories
- To write the story script so that most people
  will follow it and be interested in it
- To set the scene and give basic facts
- To lead into interviews
- To link different news items together

To be a newscaster you must:

- Explain things simply and clearly
- Use plain Standard English
- Make good notes to read from
- Speak slowly, confidently and clearly
- Keep your script on the table,
  not in front of your face
- Make eye contact with the camera
- Glance at your notes but look up to
  the camera
- Practise a few times

HELP

Speaking Standard English

- Standard English isn't 'posh', and it's nothing to do with accent.

- Standard English means keeping to words that don't exclude anyone, and avoiding, for example, local dialect words that aren't used elsewhere.

- Standard English means using the standard verbs, e.g. *we were* rather than *we was.*

- Standard English means being accurate and polite.

- Standard English means using a slightly formal tone.

Activity

- Read the news bulletins below. They are based on nursery rhymes. Try reading them as a newscaster.

  1. Can you keep a straight face?

  2. Can you keep up the tone?

  3. Can you read slowly and clearly?

  4. Can you make plenty of eye contact as you read?

- Try writing and reading your own news bulletin about a different nursery rhyme, e.g. Three Blind Mice, Jack and Jill, The Old Woman who Lived in a Shoe.

Humpty Dumpty sat on a wall
Humpty Dumpty had a great fall
All the King's horses and all the King's men
Couldn't put Humpty together again.

HUMPTY IN DEATH PLUNGE

Humpty Dumpty fell from a 40 foot wall today. The King's horses and men who were in the area tried to put the badly injured egg-man Humpty back together, but could not. He was taken to Wallsend Hospital but doctors could not revive him. Was it a tragic accident – did he fall, or worse, was he pushed?

Hey diddle, diddle
The cat and the fiddle
The cow jumped over the moon;
The little dog laughed to see such sport
And the dish ran away with the spoon.

COW IN ORBIT

Experts last night were trying to work out the biggest space mystery ever. How did a cow get into outer space? And when it reached the moon, how did it jump over? Possible links are being made with the strange theft of a spoon back on Earth. Last night a dog called Rex was helping police with their enquiries.

Unscrambling the news

The six news stories opposite have been chosen for a TV
news programme for teenage viewers. They are in the wrong
order – can you put them in the right order?

Activity

- There is one **soft news** story among the six in the list.
  Which is it? Where would you place it?

- There are five **hard news** stories. The most important story will
  go first, the next most important second, and so on. Work out
  your own running order.

- If you had twenty minutes for the programme, how would you
  divide up the time? Work out the number of minutes you
  would give to each story.

HELP

There are two types of news stories – hard and soft.

Hard news

- News stories that are just 'breaking'
- About important events

Soft news

- About less important events
- Not urgent
- Funny stories

Hard news goes before soft news. Can you see why?

1. A huge banner painted by thousands of children from all over the world has been put on show in Ireland. The banner is a mile and a half long. It tells the sad story of Korky the Killer Whale. People who are fond of animals want Korky released back into the wild.

2. England footballer Stuart Pearce has resigned as manager of Nottingham Forest. The decision comes after Forest were relegated from the Premier League. However, Pearce has said he'll continue to play for the team.

3. Three bodies found after a fire in an old warehouse have led to tearful scenes. Fans of The Sub-Zeroes fear the bodies may be those of the band members. The group used the warehouse as a studio. The cause of the fire is still not known. Police have asked anyone with information to come forward.

4. Going to the dentist is something people dread. But fillings could be a thing of the past thanks to a new invention – a tablet that you don't even have to swallow. But Dr David Ball says that people should continue to brush their teeth well. The drug is still being tested.

5. American pilot Linda Finch has reached Australia. She is following the path of Amelia Erhart, who disappeared 60 years ago when trying to fly around the world. Linda Finch is even flying the same kind of plane as Erhart.

6. Thousands of children are now left as orphans in Rwanda. Aid workers are working night and day to cope with children who are returning home to Rwanda. Five years ago thousands of families fled from their own country when war broke out. Around ten thousand children have no parents to go home to.

Links

Link sentences help newsreaders to move from one story to the next. Here are some links from a news programme:

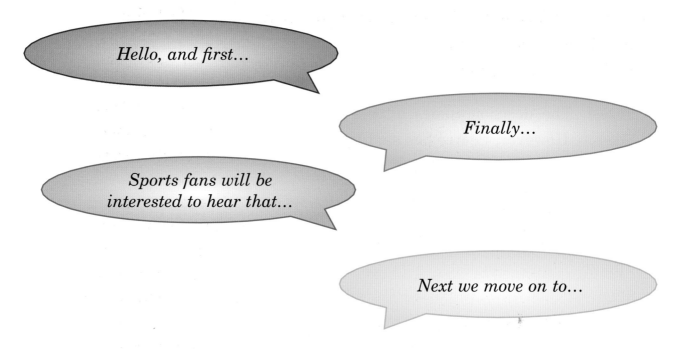

Hello, and first...

Finally...

Sports fans will be interested to hear that...

Next we move on to...

Activity

- Put each of these links before the story (on page 37) it leads into.
- Make up two more links to complete your bulletin.

Did you get it right?

Now look at the running order and times on page 44.

Activity

- Discuss anything which surprises you. Can you explain why the times are so different for each story?
- The news programme is aimed at your age group. How many of these stories would you expect to see on the adult news on the same day?

Hijack! The case of the missing bus

You are a TV reporter and this is your big chance.

A school bus has gone missing on its way to summer camp in Scotland, close to where you live. It was last seen near Lago, a small town.

You call the head teacher.

John Grant here... What? Yes, that's our bus... How many?... 42 children and three staff... Where were they going?... They were going to Glebelands summer camp for a week... No, we've had no ransom demand. I can't believe there's a problem... It's probably just a silly mistake of some kind...

HEAD TEACHER

Getting the facts

You interview local people.

They filled up with petrol about half past ten... Then they drove off... Yeah, the bus stopped and I think the brown van was in front. I couldn't see much from here. I thought maybe it was another teacher who had caught up with them for some reason.

We have no more information at this time. The bus was last seen at 10.32 this morning. Tyre tracks indicate that the bus came to a sudden halt, skidded, then moved off with another vehicle. We appeal for information from anyone who may have seen the bus, registration F745 CPH.

Some kids did come in. I clearly remember several had a Coke. They were nice kids. I'm sorry if they have been kidnapped.

HELP

Interviews

It helps if:

- You ask open questions that bring out comments rather than just 'yes' or 'no'

- You follow up any hints in what they say

- You try to get at facts, because you can't just report opinions

- You try to draw out more information

Useful phrases:

Can you tell me more about...?

Tell me more...

Why do you say that?

List two further questions you could use to draw more information from the three witnesses on page 39.

Activity

- Now put together the information for your first report. It must take exactly one minute to read aloud.

- You can use some of these sentence openings or make up your own.

A school bus has...

It was reported missing after failing to turn up at...

Shortly before disappearing, the bus stopped...

It was last seen near...

Petrol pump attendant Joe Walker told us...

Tyre tracks in the road show that...

Head teacher Mr John Grant told us that...

In the bus were... from...

Police Chief Anderson, who is in charge of the case, appealed...

The bus registration is...

This is... reporting from...

- Record your report on tape or read it aloud to the class.

Two hours later...

It is time for the next news bulletin.

What do we know about 'Free the Children'?

This is a message from 'Free the Children'. We believe this country should be free from laws. We believe every person has the right to make up their own mind how they want to live their lives. We do not believe children should be forced to attend school. Schools are prisons. Children should be free to live their lives the way they want. The children of Sackville High have been liberated by us. We demand that this tape be played on radio stations throughout the country. Only when our demands are met will the children be released...

Hmm... leader is a man called Jude Evans. Had a bad time at school, doesn't want other kids to have to put up with the same thing. He tried the same thing two years ago, but he gave himself up, and got two years in prison... came out last month.

Well, I saw this big bus and this brown van in the wood. I couldn't see too well, but I think he had a red shirt. Yes, the guy in the red shirt stuck something to a tree. I don't know what. There was a woman too, in a big blue anorak, looked like she was with him. I didn't see any kids...

I know no more than you do. Everything possible is being done. We have a hundred officers on the case. We appeal to the kidnappers to return the children to their parents...

Will we broadcast their demands? I can't say. I'll speak to Mrs Owens, who owns the station...

Activity

- You need to update your story. You can use some of these sentence openings or make up your own.

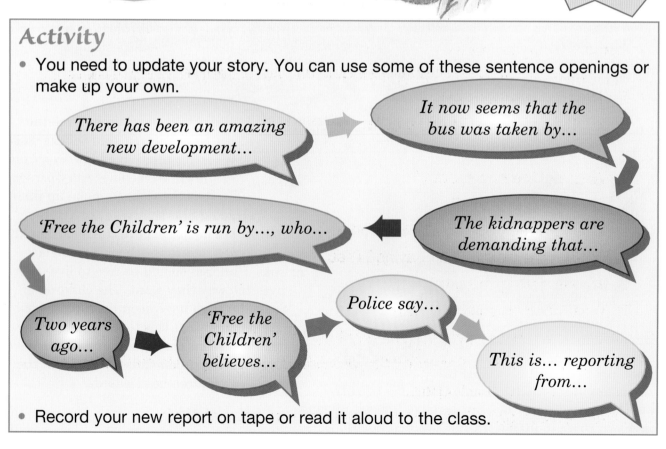

There has been an amazing new development...

It now seems that the bus was taken by...

'Free the Children' is run by..., who...

The kidnappers are demanding that...

Two years ago...

'Free the Children' believes...

Police say...

This is... reporting from...

- Record your new report on tape or read it aloud to the class.

Showdown!

Activity

- Get into groups of three.
- This is a timed activity. You have fifteen minutes to get ready for your bulletin. Start timing yourself **now**.
- Look at the picture and make notes for your bulletin.

  1. What is happening?

  2. Where is the bus exactly?

  3. Why has it stopped?

  4. What are the police marksmen doing?

  5. What is the police chief saying? (You must make this up.)

  6. Who is driving the bus?

  7. What can you see in the bus?

- Decide who will read the bulletin and help them to rehearse.
- You might start: *The Sackville High bus hijack is reaching a dramatic climax…*
- Now record your third report.
- Listen to each group's report and say what was good about it.

And next...

What do you think will happen next in the story?

- Will the hijackers give in?
- Will they make demands?
- Will they make threats?
- Will they say why they are doing it?
- Will any children be seen?
- Will there be talks?

- Will the police be allowed to help the teachers and children by bringing food and drink?
- Will the second hijacker be seen?
- How will the atmosphere change?

Activity

- Use the questions above to help you to decide what happens next.
- Make notes on your ideas.
- Make up what people such as the police chief say. Add this to your notes.
- Use your notes to write a final bulletin.

Activity

How did we do?

Discuss how your group went about the task of working out what was happening and how to deal with it.

Were you sure of your facts?

- How did you decide what was fact and what was just a guess?
- How did you word the parts that were guesses?
- Suggest some sentence starters you can use to introduce information you can't be sure of. For example:

  Some people are saying that...

Working together

- How did you deal with time pressure?
- How did you divide up the work?
- How did you decide who did what?

Original running order for 'Unscrambling the news'

Children separated from parents (six minutes)

Warehouse mystery deaths (three minutes)

Korky the Whale banner in Ireland (one minute)

Stuart Pearce resignation (two minutes)

Linda Finch round-the-world flight (four minutes)

Tooth decay report (four minutes)

UNIT THREE

Macbeth

An introduction to the main themes of the play

In this unit you will study Shakespeare's play *Macbeth*. You will get to know the plot and think about why the characters behave as they do. You will also be introduced to Shakespeare's language.

Role-play cards

Use the role-play cards on the following pages to explore some of the themes and issues in the play. When you get your card, read through the notes and discuss them with your group. Then role-play what is happening. It is better to improvise (make it up as you go along) so there is no need to write a script.

ROLE CARD A (GROUP OF 2)

Your character
You are very superstitious. You always read your horoscope. You have even been to a fortune teller.

What's happening
Your friend really wants you to go out to see a film. The film's called *Out of the Blue*. It is on for one night only. Your horoscope said to stay away from the colour blue all that day.
Act out your conversation.

ROLE CARD B (GROUP OF 4/5)

Your character
You like to be with your mates. You often meet up with them on a Saturday to go into town. Recently they've been talking about shoplifting. You think some of your mates may have done this already.

What's happening
Your mates point out something in a shop. They dare you to steal it. They tell you it's easy but you're not so sure. They try to persuade you.
Act out your conversation. Do you decide to do what they tell you, or not?

ROLE CARD C (GROUP OF 3)

Your character
Everyone at school has trendy new mobile phones. You're fed up with being the odd one out. You take some money from your dad's wallet so you can have one too.

What's happening
You arrive home from school to find both your parents waiting for you and they are not pleased. You try to explain why you took the money.
Act out your conversation.

ROLE CARD D (GROUP OF 2)

Your character

You've been going out with your boy/girlfriend for some time but have always dreamt of being famous.

What's happening

You have just had a letter offering you a place at stage school. You are very keen, but it means moving away. Your boy/girlfriend doesn't want you to go. Act out the conversation in which your boy/girlfriend tries to make you stay.

Activity

Each role-play card introduces a problem that can arise.

- Role-play the situation and show the other groups what is happening.
- Invite the rest of the class to talk about what happened in your role-play:
  - Did the characters do the right thing?
  - Are there any other solutions to the problem?
- What did you notice about how different people tried to persuade others to do something?

How ambitious are you?

> ★ **Glossary**
>
> To have an **ambition** means that there is something you really want to achieve.

> ★ **Glossary**
>
> To be **ambitious** means that you really want to be successful.

Activity

With a partner:

- Choose three of your **ambitions**.

- Talk about what you would have to do to achieve these things.

- If you knew something about the future, how would it make you feel?

- Imagine a fortune teller has just told you that you will be a famous sports person. How would it make you feel? Would it change your life?

- Have a go at **predicting** some things which might happen to others in your class.

> ★ **Glossary**
>
> **Predicting** means stating what you think might happen in the future.

Act 1, Scene 1 – the witches

The opening of Shakespeare's play is very **dramatic**. Three witches open the play. They meet in a 'desolate place'. They arrange to meet Macbeth after a battle.

A desolate place. Thunder and lightning. Enter three WITCHES

FIRST WITCH | When shall we three meet again?
In thunder, lightning, or in rain?

SECOND WITCH | When the hurly-burly's done, When the battle's lost, and won.

THIRD WITCH | That will be ere the set of sun.

FIRST WITCH | Where the place?

> ★ **Glossary**
>
> **Dramatic** means 'sudden', 'striking' or 'impressive'. Here the opening of the play is designed to grab your attention.

SECOND WITCH | Upon the heath.

THIRD WITCH | There to meet with Macbeth.

FIRST WITCH | I come, Graymalkin.

SECOND WITCH | Paddock calls.

THIRD WITCH | Anon.

ALL | Fair is foul, and foul is fair, Hover through the fog and filthy air.

Act 1, Scene 1

Activity

Work in groups of three:

- Read through the lines a few times.
- Try saying the lines in different ways: shout; whisper; speak quickly; speak slowly. Listen carefully to the words. How do they sound? What differences do you notice about each way of saying them?

Activity

- Can you find evidence in what the witches say that:
  1. They can predict the future
  2. They might be plotting something?

> ★ **Glossary**
>
> 'Graymalkin' is the name of a cat. 'Paddock' is the name of a toad. 'I come, Graymalkin' and 'Paddock calls' suggest the witches have helpers with whom they can communicate.

Reading the play

The play is split into five parts. Each part is called an Act.

You are going to carry on looking at Act 1. Read the cartoon below.

THE KING HEARS OF THE BRAVERY OF MACBETH AND BANQUO, WHO HAVE WON THE BATTLE.

ON THEIR WAY TO MEET THE KING, MACBETH AND BANQUO ARE STOPPED BY THREE WITCHES WHO PREDICT THEIR FUTURES.

HAIL MACBETH, THANE OF GLAMIS!

ALL HAIL MACBETH THANE OF CAWDOR...

...THAT SHALT BE KING HEREAFTER

THEY ALSO TELL BANQUO THAT HIS CHILDREN WILL BE KINGS.

ROSS ARRIVES WITH NEWS THAT KING DUNCAN HAS MADE MACBETH 'THANE OF CAWDOR'.

TWO TRUTHS ARE TOLD...

IN ORDER FOR THE THIRD PREDICTION TO COME TRUE, MACBETH WOULD HAVE TO KILL KING DUNCAN.

MACBETH TELLS HIS WIFE ABOUT THE WITCHES IN A LETTER. SHE WORRIES THAT HER HUSBAND IS TOO DECENT TO CARRY OUT THE MURDER.

YET DO I FEAR THY NATURE, IT IS TOO FULL O' TH' MILK OF HUMAN KINDNESS.

THAT NIGHT KING DUNCAN ARRIVES AT MACBETH'S CASTLE, AND IS WELCOMED BY LADY MACBETH.

IF WE SHOULD FAIL?

WE FAIL!

MACBETH TRIES TO PREPARE HIMSELF FOR THE MURDER. IT IS LADY MACBETH WHO FINALLY PERSUADES HIM TO GO AHEAD WITH IT.

Activity

- Try to watch a film of Act 1.
- Now read some of Act 1 as Shakespeare wrote it.

The art of persuasion

Macbeth's castle, near the Great Hall. Music and torches. Enter a butler and many servants with dishes and service over the stage. Then enter MACBETH

MACBETH   If it were done when 'tis done, then 'twere well
It were done quickly; if th'assassination
Could trammel up the consequence, and catch
With his surcease, success; that but this blow
Might be the be-all and the end-all – here,
But here, upon this bank and shoal of time,
We'd jump the life to come. But in these cases,
We still have judgement here; that we but teach
Bloody instructions, which being taught, return
To plague th'inventor; this even-handed justice
Commends th'ingredients of our poisoned chalice
To our own lips. He's here in double trust:
First, as I am his kinsman and his subject,
Strong both against the deed; then, as his host,
Who should against his murderer shut the door,
Not bear the knife myself. Besides, this Duncan
Hath borne his faculties so meek, hath been
So clear in his great office, that his virtues
Will plead like angels, trumpet-tongu'd against
The deep damnation of his taking-off;
And pity, like a naked newborn babe
Striding the blast, or heaven's cherubin hors'd
Upon the sightless couriers of the air,
Shall blow the horrid deed in every eye,
That tears shall drown the wind. I have no spur
To prick the sides of my intent, but only
Vaulting ambition which o'erleaps itself
And falls on the other.

Act 1, Scene 7

In the scene you have just read, Macbeth speaks aloud his thoughts about the murder. He wants to be king, but he doubts whether he should kill King Duncan.

Below is a list of Macbeth's arguments. Next to the arguments are lines from Macbeth's speech.

I will be killed if caught	*I am ... his subject,* *Strong both against the deed*
I am a relative of the King	*Duncan* *Hath borne his faculties so meek, hath been* *So clear in his great office*
I am his subject and should be loyal to the King	*I have no spur* *To prick the sides of my intent, but only* *Vaulting ambition*
I am his host and I should protect my guest	*this even-handed justice* *Commends th'ingredients of our poisoned* *chalice* *To our own lips*
Duncan is a good King with good qualities	*I am ... his host,* *Who should against his murderer shut the door*
I will be damned in heaven	*I am his kinsman*
I am very ambitious	*his virtues* *Will plead like angels, trumpet-tongu'd against* *The deep damnation of his taking-off*

Activity

- Match the lines in the play to the arguments.
- Which ones are for murder?
- Which ones are against murder?
- What do you think Macbeth will do?

Lady Macbeth is more determined at this point. She persuades her husband to go ahead with their plan to murder Duncan.

Macbeth says 'We will proceed no further in this business.' But by the end of the scene he has changed his mind.

Activity

- Look at the lines below. Translate them into modern English using grids like these. The first ones have been done for you.

Macbeth	Modern meaning
We will proceed no further in this business	We will not carry out our plans to murder the King
I dare do all that may become a man; Who dares do more is none	
If we should fail?	

Lady Macbeth	Modern meaning
Was hope drunk? Art thou afeard?	Have you lost your nerve?
What beast was't, then, That made you break this enterprise to me?	
We fail! But screw your courage to the sticking-place, And we'll not fail.	

- Look at this conversation between Macbeth and Lady Macbeth. What are the details of their plan?
- How does Lady Macbeth persuade Macbeth to kill the King?
- Imagine you are directing the play. Explain to the actress playing the part of Lady Macbeth how she should persuade her husband. Write down five points you would make.

MACBETH	If we should fail?
LADY MACBETH	We fail!
	But screw your courage to the sticking-place,
	And we'll not fail. When Duncan is asleep –
	Whereto the rather shall his day's hard journey
	Soundly invite him – his two chamberlains
	Will I with wine and wassail so convince
	That memory, the warder of the brain,
	Shall be a fume, and the receipt of reason
	A limbeck only: when in swinish sleep
	Their drenched natures lie as in a death,
	What cannot you and I perform upon
	The unguarded Duncan? What not put upon
	His spongy officers, who shall bear the guilt
	Of our great quell?
MACBETH	Bring forth men-children only;
	For thy undaunted mettle should compose
	Nothing but males. Will it not be received,
	When we have mark'd with blood those sleepy two
	Of his own chamber and used their very daggers,
	That they have done't?
LADY MACBETH	Who dares receive it other,
	As we shall make our griefs and clamour roar
	Upon his death?
MACBETH	I am settled, and bend up
	Each corporal agent to this terrible feat.
	Away, and mock the time with fairest show:
	False face must hide what the false heart doth know.

Act 1, Scene 7

Act 2 – murder

Activity

You have been called to investigate a crime – the murder of King Duncan.

- In groups draw up a list of suspects to be interviewed.
- Decide who will do the interviewing and who will be interviewed.
- Decide on the questions to be asked. (Remember to pretend you don't know who did it!)
- Use the table below to help you set the scene.

Who has been murdered?		
Who was in the castle at the time?		
Suspect	*Possible motives*	*Evidence*

In role-play:

- Act out one or two of your interviews.
  Remember Lady Macbeth and Macbeth are lying.

Now write a police report of your investigation. Use the photocopiable sheet below.

CRIME REPORT

Police investigation by _____

Crime _____

Suspects _____

Scene of the crime _____

Findings _____

_____

_____

_____

_____

_____

_____

_____

_____

_____

Conclusion _____

_____

_____

Signature _____

Act 3 – the banquet scene

A ghost plays an important part in Act 3, Scene 4. He has a
dramatic effect on Macbeth's behaviour.

MACBETH, NOW KING, INVITES BANQUO TO A BANQUET THAT EVENING. BANQUO IS SUSPICIOUS AND MACBETH FEARS HIM.

THOU HAST IT NOW, KING, CAWDOR, GLAMIS, ALL.

FAIL NOT OUR FEAST

UNKNOWN TO **LADY MACBETH**, MACBETH GIVES INSTRUCTIONS TO HAVE BANQUO AND HIS SON MURDERED.

BOTH OF YOU KNOW BANQUO WAS YOUR ENEMY

LADY MACBETH NOTICES HER HUSBAND'S TROUBLED MIND AND TRIES TO CALM HIM.

O, FULL OF SCORPIONS IS MY MIND, DEAR WIFE.

WHAT'S DONE IS DONE

BANQUO IS MURDERED, BUT HIS SON, FLEANCE, ESCAPES..

FLY, GOOD FLEANCE, FLY, FLY, FLY!

THE TABLE'S FULL!

AT THE BANQUET IN THE PALACE THAT NIGHT, MACBETH IS HAUNTED BY THE GHOST OF BANQUO, AND ALL THE GUESTS NOTICE HIS STRANGE BEHAVIOUR.

LADY MACBETH TRIES TO CALM HER HUSBAND AND EXCUSE HIS BEHAVIOUR. MACBETH SAYS HE WILL VISIT THE WITCHES AGAIN.

I WILL TOMORROW —TO THE WEIRD SISTERS

MY FRIENDS...

Activity

- Who is the ghost?
- Why is Macbeth so frightened of the ghost?
- How does Macbeth behave?
- If the ghost could speak, what do you think it would tell the guests?
- Complete the ghost's speech to the guests.

Staging Act 3, Scene 4

In this scene, Macbeth 'sees' the ghost of Banquo whom he has just had murdered. But the others around the table cannot see what Macbeth sees.

The table's full!

Look closely at the following section of the scene:

ROSS	Pleas't your highness
	To grace us with your royal company.
MACBETH	The table's full!
LENNOX	Here's a place reserv'd, sir.
MACBETH	Where?
LENNOX	Here, my good lord. What is't that moves your highness?
MACBETH	Which of you have done this?
LORDS	What, my good lord?
MACBETH	Thou cans't not say I did it: never shake
	Thy gory locks at me.
ROSS	Gentlemen, rise; his highness is not well.
LADY MACBETH	Sit, worthy friends: my lord is often thus,
	And hath been from his youth: pray you, keep seat;
	The fit is momentary; upon a thought
	He will again be well.

Act 3, Scene 4

Activity

You are to **direct** this part of the scene. Work with a partner. Discuss the following:

- Directors of *Macbeth* sometimes use the actor playing Banquo in this scene, others just have an empty chair and space at the table. Which solution would you use and why?

- Think about how you would put this scene on the stage, and how you would direct the actors playing each part.

★ Glossary

direct = to plan the production of a play or film

Activity

- Write a set of 'director's notes' to explain what you would do. Include details of what the actors should do (jump around, turn round, etc.) and how they should say their lines. (See the Help Box on page 60.)

- If you are able, work with a group of other pupils playing these roles. Set the scene out as you wish it to be, remembering your decision about using an actor to play Banquo's ghost or not. Direct the scene, stopping the action to help actors get into their role. Help them to practise saying their lines in different ways.

- You should aim to direct a scene that shows Macbeth as a person who is becoming tormented by the murder of his best friend, and shows how the other lords and Macbeth's wife can't understand what is upsetting him so much.

- Compare the different versions: which works best and why?

HELP

Director's notes

- Draw a sketch of how you would set out the stage and where different characters would be sitting.

- Photocopy the section of the scene from your copy of the play and write notes next to the lines to show what the actor should do and how they should say their line.

For example:

MACBETH   Which of you have done this?

Stares at the empty space, eyes popping, then looks suddenly at everyone

Note of panic in his voice, shouting by the end of the line

Act 4 – the witches' spell

In Act 4, Scene 1 the witches brew a spell. The spell is to show Macbeth the future. Their spell is made up of some very strange ingredients!

A desolate place near Forres. Thunder. Enter the three WITCHES

FIRST WITCH
Thrice the brindled cat hath mewed.

SECOND WITCH
Thrice and once the hedge-pig whined.

THIRD WITCH
Harpier cries, "Tis time, 'tis time.'

FIRST WITCH
Round about the cauldron go;
In the poisoned entrails throw.
Toad, that under cold stone
Days and nights has thirty-one
Sweltered venom sleeping got,
Boil thou first i'th'charmed pot.

ALL
Double, double, toil and trouble;
Fire burn, and cauldron bubble.

SECOND WITCH
Fillet of a fenny snake,
In the cauldron boil and bake:
Eye of newt, and toe of frog,
Wool of bat, and tongue of dog,
Adder's fork, and blind-worm's sting,
Lizard's leg, and howlet's wing,
For a charm of powerful trouble,
Like a hell-broth, boil and bubble.

ALL
Double, double, toil and trouble,
Fire burn, and cauldron bubble.

THIRD WITCH
Scale of dragon, tooth of wolf,
Witches' mummy, maw and gulf
Of the ravined salt-sea shark,
Root of hemlock, digged i'th'dark;
Liver of blaspheming Jew,
Gall of goat, and slips of yew
Slivered in the moon's eclipse;
Nose of Turk, and Tartar's lips,
Finger of birth-strangled babe,
Ditch-delivered by a drab,
Make the gruel thick and slab.
Add thereto a tiger's chawdron
For th'ingredients of our cauldron.

ALL
Double, double, toil and trouble,
Fire burn, and cauldron bubble.

SECOND WITCH
Cool it with a baboon's blood,
Then the charm is firm and good.

Act 4, Scene 1

Activity

- Copy the cauldron below. Draw and label all the ingredients of the witches' spell. You may need to look up some of the words in a dictionary.

- Invent your own spell written in rhyming couplets.

  Try to write at least *eight* lines.

HELP

Rhyming couplets

Rhyming couplets are made when each pair of lines rhymes, for example:

Eye of newt, and toe of frog,

Wool of bat, and tongue of dog,

Adder's fork, and blind-worm's sting,

Lizard's leg, and howlet's wing

Each pair of lines is called a **couplet** (from the word 'couple').

For your spell, you could use modern ingredients or think of different creatures.

Write a list of ingredients first. Then choose ones that rhyme.

More predictions

The witches give Macbeth a glimpse of the future.

They also give him three more predictions.

Activity

- Read the cartoon below, then discuss these questions in pairs:

  1. How do you think Macbeth feels after hearing the three predictions?

  2. Why do you think Macbeth decides to kill Macduff's family? After all, they are no threat to him.

  3. How much has Macbeth changed since we first met him? He was described as 'brave Macbeth' at the start of the play. How would you describe him now?

Act 5 – bad news

Ross has to tell Macduff what has happened to his family. He delays in telling him – why might that be? Think about how you would break some bad news to a friend.

Activity

- Write your own script of the conversation between Ross and Macduff.
- What do you think Ross would say to Macduff about the death of his wife and son?
- Now act out your script with a partner.
- Compare your script and how you acted it out with another pair.
- What were some of the differences?

OUT, DAMNED SPOT...

LADY MACBETH IS NOW SERIOUSLY DISTURBED BY ALL THAT HAS HAPPENED. SHE IS FOUND SLEEPWALKING, TRYING TO WASH IMAGINARY SPOTS OF BLOOD FROM HER HANDS.

A LARGE ARMY IS GATHERING NEARBY. MALCOLM GIVES ORDERS THAT EVERY SOLDIER MUST CUT DOWN A BRANCH SO MACBETH CANNOT TELL THEIR NUMBERS.

AT DUNSINANE CASTLE..

THE QUEEN, MY LORD, IS DEAD!

METHOUGHT THE WOOD BEGAN TO MOVE!

MACBETH IS TOLD THAT LADY MACBETH IS DEAD. HE STILL THINKS HE CANNOT BE CONQUERED, BUT IS THEN TOLD THAT BIRNAM WOOD IS MOVING

EVENTUALLY MACBETH AND MACDUFF FIGHT. MACBETH REALISES HIS MISTAKES WHEN MACDUFF TELLS HIM HE WAS BORN BY CAESAREAN.

MACDUFF KILLS MACBETH AND CUTS OFF HIS HEAD.

MALCOLM IS HAILED THE NEW KING OF SCOTLAND.

The wood comes to Dunsinane

Enter a Messenger.

MACBETH   Thou comest to use thy
                 tongue; thy story quickly.

MESSENGER   Gracious my lord,
                 I should report that which I
                 say I saw,
                 But know not how to do it.

MACBETH   Well, say, sir.

MESSENGER   As I did stand my watch upon
                 the hill,
                 I look'd toward Birnam, and
                 anon, methought,
                 The wood began to move.

MACBETH   Liar and slave!

MESSENGER   Let me endure your wrath, if 't
                 be not so:
                 Within this three mile may you
                 see it coming;
                 I say, a moving grove.

MACBETH   If thou speak'st false,
                 Upon the next tree shalt thou
                 hang alive,
                 Till famine cling thee: if thy
                 speech be sooth,

I care not if thou dost for me
    as much.
I pull in resolution, and begin
To doubt the equivocation of
    the fiend
That lies like truth: 'Fear not,
    till Birnam wood
Do come to Dunsinane': and
    now a wood
Comes toward Dunsinane.
Arm, arm, and out!
If this which he avouches
    does appear,
There is nor flying hence nor
    tarrying here.
I 'gin to be aweary of the sun,
And wish the estate o' the
    world were now undone.
Ring the alarum-bell! Blow,
    wind! come, wrack!
At least we'll die with harness
    on our back.

Act 5, Scene 5

Activity

How is Macbeth feeling here:

confident

brave

fearful?

The witches predict the following:

1. Macbeth will be Thane of Cawdor
2. Macbeth will become King
3. Macbeth should beware Macduff

4. Nobody 'of woman born shall harm Macbeth'

5. Macbeth will never be defeated until Birnam wood comes to 'high Dunsinane hill'.

- How have predictions 3, 4 and 5 come true?

- How does Macbeth react when he finds out that predictions 4 and 5 do not mean that he is safe?

Macbeth fights Macduff

They fight.

MACBETH   Thou losest labour:
As easy mayst thou the intrenchant air
With thy keen sword impress as make me bleed:
Let fall thy blade on vulnerable crests:
I bear a charmed life, which must not yield
To one of woman born.

MACDUFF   Despair thy charm;
And let the angel whom thou still hast served
Tell thee, Macduff was from his mother's womb
Untimely ripp'd.

MACBETH   Accursed be that tongue that tells me so,
For it hath cow'd my better part of man!
And be these juggling fiends no more believed,
That palter with us in a double sense;
That keep the word of promise to our ear,
And break it to our hope. I'll not fight with thee.

MACDUFF   Then yield thee, coward.

Act 5, Scene 8

Activity

- Do you think Macbeth knows his luck has finally run out?
  Find the line where he seems to give up.
- Read on to 'And damn'd be him that first cries, "Hold, enough!".'
  Why doesn't Macbeth give in? Why does he decide to die fighting?
- What do you think of this decision? Do you admire him or not?

You have looked at the whole play. You have worked on the activities in the first part of this unit. Use the 'Focus On ...' sheets on the following pages to look at some of the characters more closely.

You could split into groups to look at different characters and then report back.

Focus on Macbeth

Derek Jacobi as Macbeth, RSC (Royal Shakespeare Company)

Activity

- What crimes does Macbeth commit during the play?

- Look at the list of words below which are used in the play to describe Macbeth (use a dictionary if you are not sure of their meanings). Which do you agree with? Which don't you agree with? Why?

brave	avaricious	wicked	mad
tyrant	false	devilish	hell hound
black	deceitful	fiend	coward
devil	malicious	monster	butcher

- How does the character of Macbeth change throughout the play? On a separate sheet, copy the graph below. Fill it in to show how Macbeth's fortunes and character change. Use some of the adjectives from the list above. It has been started for you:

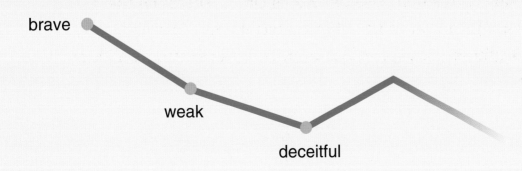

Activity

- Put the following events into order to show what happens to Macbeth.

    1. Macbeth murders King Duncan.

    2. He arranges the murder of Lady Macduff and her children.

    3. He wins the battle and is honoured by King Duncan.

    4. He prepares for battle. He is told the Queen is dead and Birnam wood moves.

    5. He is crowned King of Scotland.

    6. He meets the three witches.

    7. He arranges Banquo's murder.

    8. He is beheaded by Macduff.

    9. He revisits the three witches.

    10. He fights Macduff and believes he cannot be harmed.

    11. He sees Banquo's ghost.

- Match these lines from the play with the events above.

    A. For brave Macbeth – well he deserves that name

    B. I will tomorrow to the weird sisters

    C. Banquo, thy soul's flight, if it find Heaven, must find it out tonight

    D. The sovereignty will fall upon Macbeth

    E. Behold where stands th' usurper's cursed head

    F. All hail, Macbeth, that shalt be King hereafter

    G. I have done the deed

    H. Give to th' edge o' th' sword his wife, his babes

    I. I bear a charmed life which must not yield to one of woman born

    J. The table's full

    K. The Queen, my Lord, is dead

Focus on Lady Macbeth

Activity

At the end of Act 2

Lady Macbeth persuades her husband, Macbeth, to carry out the murder of King Duncan.

- What sort of person is she?
- How would you describe her relationship with Macbeth?
- How does she react to the murder?

At the end of Act 3

- Which of the words below best describe Lady Macbeth?

  ambitious   persuasive

  in charge   brave

  ruthless   clever

- Can you think of any other words to describe Lady Macbeth?
- Can you find any extracts in the play which support your view of Lady Macbeth?

Cheryl Campbell as Lady Macbeth, RSC

At the end of Act 5

- Lady Macbeth is very influential in the play. Would Macbeth have carried out the murders without her?
- At the start she seems a strong character. Later she is tormented by what they have done. Put the following sentences in order to describe what happens to Lady Macbeth.

  1. Lady Macbeth sleepwalks and tries to wash imaginary blood from her hands.
  2. She plans to murder King Duncan.
  3. She dies.
  4. She helps to make the King's servants look guilty.
  5. She tries to explain Macbeth's strange behaviour at the banquet.

- Now match these quotations to the events described above:

  A. I'll gild the faces of the grooms withal
  B. Pray you, keep seat. The fit is momentary
  C. What, will these hands ne'er be clean?
  D. He that's coming must be provided for
  E. The Queen, my lord, is dead

- At the end of the play she is described as a 'fiend-like queen'. Do you think this is a fair description of Lady Macbeth?

Focus on Banquo

Banquo bravely fights alongside Macbeth at the beginning of the play. He is also with Macbeth when they meet the witches for the first time. He is told that his descendants will be kings yet he is not tempted to do evil like Macbeth.

Christopher Ravenscroft as Banquo, RSC

Activity

- Which of these statements below might explain Banquo's behaviour?

  1. He's content with what he has.
  2. He's loyal to King Duncan.
  3. He doesn't believe in witches.
  4. He has no scheming wife to persuade him.
  5. He is a good man who would never do wrong.

- Can you think of any other reasons?

- What sort of person is Banquo? Can you find evidence in the play to suggest that he is:

  loyal

  brave

  honest?

- Banquo provides a contrast to Macbeth. Put in order the events that happen to Banquo.

  1. He meets the three witches.
  2. He is seen as a ghost by Macbeth.
  3. He is welcomed by King Duncan after winning the battle.
  4. He is suspicious of Macbeth's actions.
  5. He is murdered but his son Fleance escapes.

- Now match these quotations with the events above.

  A. I fear thou playd'st most foully for 't

  B. O, treachery! Fly, good Fleance, fly, fly, fly!

  C. What are these, so withered and so wild in their attire?

  D. Noble Banquo, let me enfold thee and hold thee to my heart

  E. Thy bones are marrowless, thy blood is cold

Focus on Macduff

Macduff is suspicious. He is worried about the way Macbeth is ruling Scotland. He goes to England to ask for help. He returns with an army to fight Macbeth.

Peter Guiness as Macduff, RSC

Activity

- Put the following events in order.
  1. He kills Macbeth and cuts off his head.
  2. He tells Macbeth he was born by caesarean.
  3. The witches warn Macbeth to watch out for him.
  4. He discovers King Duncan murdered at Macbeth's castle.
  5. He goes to England to ask for help.
  6. He is told that his wife and children have been murdered while he was in England.

- Now match these quotations to the events above.
  A. Thither Macduff is gone to pray the holy King upon his aid
  B. Ring the alarum bell! Murder and treason
  C. Behold where stands th' usurper's cursed head
  D. Beware Macduff. Beware the Thane of Fife
  E. Macduff was from his mother's womb untimely ripped
  F. What, all my pretty chickens and their dam at one fell swoop?

Writing about *Macbeth*

In this unit you have looked carefully at the play *Macbeth*. You have followed the plot. You have understood how Macbeth's ambition destroyed him in the end. You have used role-play to help you think about the characters and what happens to them. Watching the play will have helped you to see how it all fits together. Choose one of the following three questions to use to write about the play:

1. What drives Macbeth to kill the King and keep on killing?
2. Do you think Macbeth is man or monster?
3. What is the most exciting part of the play, and why?

HELP

Writing about the play

- You are asked for **your** views. Say what you think and back your views up with **evidence**. Find key lines in the play that you can use.

- Don't retell the story.

- Plan your writing into paragraphs. Each paragraph should be based on one key idea and use at least one quotation as evidence.

- Start each paragraph with a topic sentence that expresses your main idea. Then give reasons and evidence from the text.

- Link your paragraphs by using phrases such as:

  'There are several reasons why I think...'

  'Firstly...'

  'Another reason is...'

  'Although some people argue that...'

  'Others think that...'

  'By the end of the play...'

  'In conclusion...'

Preparing for the Checkpoint Tests

Getting ready for tests

The Checkpoint English tests assess your progress in reading and writing. There are two papers: Paper 1 tests your reading and writing of non-narrative texts. Paper 2 tests your reading and writing of narrative texts. This unit will help you to prepare for these tests.

The reading tests

You will be expected to read two or three pieces of text such as:

- A piece of fiction
- An information text
- Someone writing about their experiences, e.g. travel writing
- Someone writing about their opinions

You have to show that you can:

- Understand what a text is about
- Read between the lines
- Express a view about it
- Justify your views with evidence
- Explain how the writer made you think or feel as you did

The writing tests

In the writing tests you may be asked to write:

- A story
- A letter
- Information
- An article
- A description
- A point of view

You have to show that you can:

- Adapt your writing for a special audience
- Fit your style to the purpose
- Express yourself clearly
- Make your writing interesting and readable
- Spell and punctuate correctly

Answering reading questions
Give yourself thinking time

Avoid mistakes by thinking first. Take time to:

- Read the passage to get a general understanding
- Read the questions. Work out what they want.
  Find key words in them
- Read the text again, with the questions in mind
- Underline, circle or highlight useful words to help you answer the questions
- Work out how much time you have and break up your time to get most marks

HELP

Slow readers

Are you a slow reader?

Do you tend to run out of time in tests?

- Save time by *scanning* the passage the first time you read it. Don't read every word – just enough to get a general understanding.
- Read the questions carefully.
- Read the passage properly the second time and look for the answers as you go.

HELP

Annotating the text

- Find words and phrases you can use in your answers.
- Choose the quotations that best support your answer.
- When you spot something that will help with a question, write the number of the question next to it.
- Write words in the margin if you have ideas for your answer.
- You could use different colour codes for different questions.

Non-fiction reading (Paper 1)

Answering questions about factual texts is very similar to answering questions about stories, but there is more to say about the choice of information and how it is structured.

The examiner is interested in:

- The choice of words
- Important details
- Evidence
- Hearing how the evidence proves a point
- Points expressed clearly
- Seeing how the writer created the effect on the reader

Remember what to do

- Read the passage.
- Read the questions.
- Read the passage looking for useful details to answer the questions.
- Annotate the passage.
- Plan your time to pick up marks.
- Use evidence to support your points.
- Explain why your evidence proves the point.

Answering summary questions

When answering summary questions, remember to:

- Keep focused on the question when reading the passage.
- Highlight or underline all the sections that are relevant to the question.
- Do not write an introduction.
- Use your own words and be as concise as possible.

Practice

Spend 35 minutes reading and answering the questions.

Read this newspaper report about an encounter with a wild animal.

Sharon Stone set up what she thought was the perfect early birthday surprise for her husband, Phil Bronstein. The Hollywood star of the film *Basic Instinct* arranged for him to go into the Komodo dragon enclosure at Los Angeles Zoo.

Phil Bronstein, executive editor of the *San Francisco Chronicle*, had always been fascinated by the Komodo dragon, the world's largest lizard.

So that the three-metre-long beast would not mistake his shoes for rats, he was advised to take them off before entering the Komodo dragon's cage with a keeper. He certainly got his surprise: the dragon immediately pounced on his bare foot clamping its saw-like teeth into his flesh and thrashing the foot from side to side. The result was a broken toe, lacerations and several severed tendons. Mr Bronstein escaped by crawling through the tiny feeding door in the cage and was taken to Cedars-Sinai Medical Centre where he underwent surgery and was treated with antibiotics.

The zoo has two Komodo dragons on display in separate cages. A spokeswoman for the zoo, which often organises behind-the-scenes tours for celebrities, said that the lizard that had bitten Mr Bronstein was not usually aggressive.

'This was totally unexpected. He has been very, very tame in the past. Our zookeeper has gone in with him several times,' Lora LaMarca told the *Los Angeles Times*. 'We have a number of celebrities who want to go behind the scenes and Mr Bronstein had a fondness for these dragons, according to his wife.'

She said the zoo would now be reviewing its policy of allowing celebrities to enter the enclosure of the four-year-old dragon.

The dragons were moved to the zoo three years ago after being confiscated from people who were trying to smuggle them into the country from the animals' homeland, the Komodo Islands of Indonesia. They are not venomous but their bite can be poisonous because their teeth harbour bacteria.

Activity

- Answer these questions.

  1. Explain (i) why Sharon Stone thought that going into a dragon's cage would make a 'perfect' type of surprise for her husband and (ii) what the real surprise was for everyone present.

  2. In your own words give three ways in which the dragon attacked Phil Bronstein.

  3. Give the meaning of each of the following words as used in the passage:

     display — on show

     celebrities — Known, celebrated people

     reviewing — seeing and Thinking about changing

     confiscated — Taken away

- Write a summary of what you have learned about the nature and habits of the Komodo dragon from this article. Write about 80 words and use your own words as far as possible.

Narrative reading (Paper 2)

Activity

One of the texts that you read for your Paper 2 exam will be an example of fiction – a story.

- Read the passage on pages 79–80 in which two men take a rest before going on to the ranch where they are to work as labourers. George walks in front. Lennie always walks behind.

The evening of the hot day started a little wind gently moving among the leaves. The shade climbed up the hills toward the top. On the sand-banks the rabbits sat as quiet as little grey, sculptured stones. And then from the direction of the state highway came the sound of footsteps on crisp sycamore leaves. The rabbits hurried noiselessly for cover. A heron laboured up into the air and pounded down-river. For a moment the place was lifeless, and then two men emerged from the path and came into the opening by the green pool. The first man was small and quick, dark of face, with restless eyes and sharp strong features. Every part of him was defined: small, strong hands, slender arms, a thin and bony nose. Behind him walked his opposite, a huge man, shapeless of face, with large pale eyes, with wide, sloping shoulders; and he walked heavily, dragging his feet a little, the way a bear drags his paws. His arms did not swing at his sides, but hung loosely and only moved at all because of the heavy weight of his hands. They had walked in single file down the path, and even in the open one stayed behind the other. Both were dressed in denim trousers and in denim coats with brass buttons. Both wore black shapeless hats and both carried tight blanket rolls slung over their shoulders.

The first man, George, stopped short in the clearing, and the follower nearly ran over him. He took off his hat and wiped the sweatband with his forefinger and snapped the moisture off. His huge companion dropped his blankets and flung himself down and drank from the surface of the green pool; drank with long gulps, snorting into the water like a horse. The small man stepped nervously beside him.

'Lennie!' he said sharply. 'Lennie, for God's sake don't drink so much.' Lennie continued to snort into the pool. The small man leaned over and shook him by the shoulder. 'Lennie. You gonna be sick like you was last night.'

Lennie dipped his whole head under, hat and all, and then he sat up on the bank and the water from his hat dripped down on his blue coat and ran down his back. 'Tha's good,' he said. 'You drink some, George. You take a good big drink.' He smiled happily.

George unslung his bundle and dropped it gently on the bank. 'I ain't sure it's good water,' he said. 'Looks kinda scummy.'

Lennie dabbled his big paw in the water and wiggled his fingers so the water arose in little splashes; rings widened across the pool to the other side and came back again. Lennie watched them go. 'Look, George. Look what I done.' *not clever 2*

George knelt beside the pool and drank from his hand with quick scoops. 'Tastes all right,' he admitted. 'Don't really seem to be running, though. You never oughta drink water when it ain't running, Lennie,' he said hopelessly. 'You'd drink out of a gutter if you was thirsty.' *unhygienic 3* He threw a scoop of water into his face and rubbed it about with his hand, under his chin and round the back of his neck. Then he replaced his hat, pushed himself back from the river, drew up his knees and embraced them. Lennie, who had been watching, imitated George exactly. *2* He pushed himself back, drew up his knees, embraced them, looked over to George to see that he had it just right. He pulled his hat down a little more over his eyes, the way George's hat was.

From *Of Mice and Men* by John Steinbeck

Activity

- Give four phrases that show the peacefulness of the place described in lines 1 to 8. Then, for each of your answers, explain how the writer's choice of words expresses this sense of peacefulness.

- Give four ways in which the writer suggests that George is the leader. Support each of your answers with a quotation from the passage.

- Give four words or phrases that describe Lennie's character. Give an explanation of each of your answers.

There will usually be three questions to answer after
you have read the text. You may be asked about:

- Characters and why they do what they do
- The mood and how it is created
- Things that are suggested but not stated
- How the writer makes you feel towards the people,
  events or place

You may be asked to comment on:

- The writer's choice of words
- How the story is told
- The choice of details

Avoiding pitfalls

Examiners are agreed that the most common mistakes are:

- Retelling the story, and hoping the answer is obvious
- Passing an opinion but not backing it up with evidence
- Giving evidence but not explaining how it proves the point
- Talking about the characters as if they are real people,
  forgetting they are cleverly created by the writer

Giving evidence

This is how to make good use of evidence:

- Make a point
- Provide evidence, a quotation if you can
- Explain why that proves the point

Using quotations

- Keep the quotation short (but do not write just the line number and expect the examiner to find it).

- Put quotation marks before and after it.

- Choose the most important words and details.

- Include the quotation in a sentence if you can.

- Short quotations should be built into sentences, taking the place of your own words, like this:

Lennie followed George and 'imitated George exactly'.

Answering writing questions
Writing narrative

What people do well when they write stories:
- Openings
- Events
- Action

What people tend to forget:
- Paragraph breaks
- The importance of working towards the ending
- Keeping the reader curious about what will happen next
- What the characters are thinking and feeling

Tips for top marks:
- Give insights into the minds of the characters and say what they are feeling
- Plan the ending
- Concentrate on using words and details that create mood and character

Quick plans for writing non-narrative (Paper 1)

Writing non-narrative is easier than writing stories because you don't have to invent a plot, and the style is often more direct. The thing that is difficult is deciding how to organise your material.

Use your planning time to do three things:

1. Group the ideas or information into clusters
2. Decide on the order
3. Create opening lines for each section

1. Group the ideas or information into clusters	**Should first aid or swimming be put on the timetable in every secondary school?**	
	Pros swimming Useful on holiday Reduces risk of drowning Healthy exercise Aids co-ordination **Pros first aid** Might save a life Useful in emergencies Needed for some jobs, e.g. nursing, driver	**Cons swimming** Something else would have to go Not all schools have a pool Time to dress/undress Problems with people forgetting kit **Cons first aid** Can learn this outside Cost of materials for practice Training staff to teach it
2. Decide on the order	1 Introduction – finding time for useful skills in packed curriculum 2 Pros swimming 3 Pros first aid	4 Cons swimming 5 Cons first aid 6 Conclusion – swimming if we have to choose, but could fit both in a Life Skills course
3. Create opening lines for each section	1 School is meant to prepare pupils for life ahead, yet… 2 It's hard to imagine a subject for which there is a better case for inclusion in the curriculum than swimming… 3 But there is another subject worthy of being taught to all pupils, and that is first aid…	

Try planning for the following topic.

Either:

• The state should pay wages for housework.

Or:

• National law should be abolished in favour of international law.

The **very quick** method of planning non-narrative writing is just to plan the sentence starters.

Quick story planning (Paper 2)

Spend a few minutes on planning. Use this story sequence to help you:

1. Start the story	Get the story going. Set the scene. Introduce a character or two. Set the mood.
2. Introduce a problem	Make something happen that will upset the way things are – something interesting, so you want to see how people will deal with it.
3. Complicate matters	Make life harder for the characters, so they are in a fix.
4. Bring it to a crisis	Bring matters to a head – a clash, a crash, a row, an embarrassment, something that can't be ignored.
5. Make people adjust to it	Show how the characters react, or try to sort things out.
6. Resolve the problem	Bring the story to a fitting conclusion – perhaps reward the good and punish the bad. Settle matters.

Learn the six stages in order:

- Start
- Problem
- Complicate
- Crisis
- Adjust
- Resolve

(Some people learn **SPACE CAR** as a way of remembering.
Use it if it works for you.)

Try planning this story. The first three stages have been done. You plan the last three stages.

1. Start the story	New pupil starts school. We become friends. Lots in common.
2. Introduce a problem	But I notice he's the last into school, the first out and never there at lunch times or breaks. I ask him round to my house.
3. Complicate matters	He disappears altogether. A big search is started. His address is false. His phone number doesn't exist.
4. Bring it to a crisis	
5. Make people adjust to it	
6. Resolve the problem	

Here is another plan. This time the last two stages are done, and you have to make up the first four.

1. Start the story	
2. Introduce a problem	
3. Complicate matters	
4. Bring it to a crisis	
5. Make people adjust to it	I realise that some of my friends are only interested in me for my looks, and that some people I never noticed before are actually quite nice. Jackie is one of these. I apologise to her, because now I know how she feels.
6. Resolve the problem	Next morning, I'm back to normal. But something has changed: I have new friends, and a better attitude.

Now use the grid to plan a story of your own.

Either:

- A story about an unusual friendship.

Or:

- My dog can talk!

Tips for the examination

1. You know the mistakes you always make. Think of a way of remembering them and write it at the top of your examination paper in pencil. This will remind you to check.

2. Learn the spellings you think you might need.

3. Proofread. It helps to read your sentences in reverse order: last sentence first, then the one before that and so on.

4. Remember to start a new paragraph when you:
   - Start a new topic
   - Move to a different time
   - Shift to a new place
   - Someone else starts to speak

5. Vary your sentences. Try the following.
   - Begin your sentence with an adverb ending in –ly, e.g. *Warily, she looked round the corner.*
   - Embed a subordinate clause, e.g. *The man, who had been lurking in the shadows, sidled away.*
   - Begin with a preposition, e.g. *Through the door stormed the teacher.*
   - Use a short sentence. This is especially effective if it follows a number of long ones, e.g. *It stopped.*

Activity

- Can you suggest five ways in which this student's writing could be improved?

> *Mikey woke up and looked out of his window it was raining. He was late for school. He got up and got dressed. He didn't have time for breakfast. If he missed the bus again he would get another detention. When he got to school the bell had just gone great, Mikey thought. Then Mr Spencer came round the corner.*

UNIT FIVE

Scandal

In two minds...

Chris and Raheela have a problem. They want to accuse David
Watson of causing pollution. If they do he won't want to give
their school any computers. Which is more important:

- To have a computer for everyone in the school?
- To have a clean river?

Activity

Look at the pictures above. Write down as many arguments as you can for:

- Having a computer for everyone in the school
- Having a clean river

Getting your message across

Look at these two speeches:

A. Ladies and gentlemen, if the school has more computers we'll get better results and better jobs.

B. Can you imagine what a marvellous thing it will be for Redwood School, ladies and gentlemen, if every child in every class can have the use of their own computer? What happens at the moment?

In every IT lesson we have to cram four pupils round one computer. As a result, three out of four students are bored. With one computer to one student everyone will be learning at a much faster rate. Our exam results are bound to improve.

Which speech is more effective? Why?

HELP

Making a point

- Posing questions makes people think.
- Paint a picture of the good that will be done.
- Say exactly what you are asking for.
- Explain your thinking.
- Help people to see how they personally will benefit.
- Explain your point two or three times, to help it sink in.

Activity

In a group, remember some times when you have listened to someone else trying to persuade you. For example:

Someone asking a favour
A politician making a speech
A parent trying to make you see sense

- How did they get your attention?
- What tactics did they use to persuade you?
- What things put you off?

HELP

Appealing to listeners

A good speaker knows what people are listening for. For example:

- How will it benefit me?
- Is this something I *should* do?
- What will happen if I don't?
- How will it affect me, good or bad?
- Can I trust the speaker?

Persuaders also know that they can use:

- Flattery
- Threats
- Bribery
- Guilt

Activity

- Work in groups to plan two speeches:

Speech 1

1. Start planning the speech for a cleaner river like this:
   - *Ladies and gentlemen, think of all the advantages of a clean river.*
   - *Think of the anglers, who fish in the river…*

2. Think of two or three points to make about anglers, for example:
   - *fish will thrive in clean water*
   - *clean riverbank*
   - *will encourage more anglers*

3. Think of two or three points to make about the view.
   - *And what about people who just like a beautiful view…*

4. Think of two or three points to make about children.
   - *Then there are children who like to paddle or swim…*

Speech 2

1. Make up some sentence starters for Speech 2 in favour of more computers in school.

2. Under each sentence starter, think of two or three points to make.

- Choose which speech to make, and rehearse it.
- When all the groups have made their speeches, the class can vote on the best speech.
- In groups, discuss what makes a good speech.

Which speech is most effective? Why?

THE TESTS SHOW THE SAME RESULT. THEY TRY TO CHECK THE SAMPLES THEY TOOK THE DAY BEFORE

Does the story stand up?

Chris and Raheela get their chance to talk to the boss. But before they go in they think hard:

What do they know that is **fact** – something they **know** to be true?

What, on the other hand, is **opinion** – something that **might** be true?

Activity

- Look at the statements below.
- Discuss each statement in pairs. Decide whether each statement is fact or opinion.
- On a copy of this grid, tick the correct column.

Statement	Fact	Opinion
There are dead fish in the river.		
The pollution comes from the factory.		
Pollution is killing the fish.		
Stopping pollution is less important than a drug for old people.		
Stopping pollution is more important than a drug for old people.		
There have been cases of tummy upset.		
Clean water is more important than computers for the school.		

Chris and Raheela put their point of view to the radio station's boss and Mike, the legal expert.

Activity

- Split into groups of four. Choose who will take the parts of Raheela, Chris, the Radio Station Boss and Mike.

- Act out the discussion. Raheela and Chris must persuade Mike and the Radio Station Boss to report the story.

HELP

- Be polite and tactful.
- Be firm but don't be aggressive.
- Say what you want and why you want it.
- Tell them why you think they should help you.

THE NEXT DAY
I'LL TELL YOU WHAT WE'LL DO. WE'LL PUT AN ARTICLE IN THE SCHOOL MAGAZINE!

GREAT IDEA! BUT WE'D BETTER NOT GO OVER THE TOP.

I'LL TELL YOU WHAT. WE'LL BOTH WRITE ARTICLES, THEN WE'LL SEE WHICH ONE IS THE BEST.

How far can we go?

Chris and Raheela both write articles. Chris blames David Watson's factory for the pollution. Raheela is more careful. She describes the pollution as a mystery. She doesn't jump to any conclusions.

Extracts from the two articles are given on the next page. Can you tell who wrote each line?

Activity

- Using a photocopy of page 109, cut up the boxes.

- Put the lines under the right headline and in the right order.

- You do not have the parts of the articles which tell you about the factory owned by David Watson.

    1. What do you think Raheela's article would say about the factory?

    2. What would Chris's article say?

- Write an extra paragraph for each article, which fits in with the approach of the rest.

---

by Raheela Khan

Ten-year-old Darren Atkins was another sufferer, after taking a two-minute paddle.

A large number of dead fish have been found in the river. What has happened? It is a mystery.

Tests on river water prove that aluminium sulphate is the killer.

WATSON FACTORY POLLUTING RIVER

Other strange things have happened in the past few weeks.

Thousands of fish are dying in the river. They have been killed by poison. The poison is a chemical called aluminium sulphate.

We have heard that some people have had upset stomachs. They all live along the river.

MYSTERY OF DEAD FISH

An outbreak of upset stomachs is almost certainly linked to aluminium sulphate.

by Chris Bloom

Samples of the river water have been tested. They show very high levels of aluminium sulphate.

A ten-year-old boy, Darren Atkins, also came out in a rash after paddling in the river.

Several other incidents of pollution have been reported.

Panic stations

PEOPLE GET TO HEAR OF THE ARTICLE IN THE SCHOOL MAGAZINE. SUDDENLY PEOPLE COME FORWARD WITH MORE SYMPTOMS.

WATER RUNS ORANGE

'I JUST HAD A SHOWER AND THIS HAPPENED....'

I CAN'T EVEN REMEMBER IF I CAME BY CAR, OR ON THE TRAIN...

CAR PARK

OTHERS GET SEVERE STOMACH PAINS

SUDDENLY THERE IS FEAR IN THE AREA

DO NOT APPROACH

DANGER

CROWDS GATHER AT THE GATES OF THE FACTORY

ALL THIS IS HARD FOR 13 YR OLD CLAIRE WATSON

FOR MONTHS SHE HAS LISTENED TO HER PARENTS' ROWS

A PURIFICATION PLANT WOULD COST US £5 MILLION. WE'D BE OUT OF BUSINESS!

WE'RE DOING ALL WE CAN!

BUT LOOK WHAT'S HAPPENING TO THE FISH!

WELL YOU AREN'T DOING ENOUGH!

THERE'S NO PROOF IT'S US!

THE REPORTER 10P

MORE STOMACH UPSETS

CLAIRE, I REALLY DON'T WANT YOU GOING NEAR THE RIVER AT THE MOMENT.

THAT'S RIDICULOUS, CLAIRE. YOU CAN GO WHERE YOU LIKE!

AND IT'S ALL BECAUSE YOU WOULDN'T PAY FOR A PURIFICATION PLANT

BUT I'VE TOLD YOU! WE'D GO OUT OF BUSINESS!

Claire's diary

Claire, alone in her room, keeps a diary in which she records her thoughts. Whose side should she be on?

It is very difficult for Claire to make up her mind. She knows that the factory employs hundreds of people in the town. They would lose their jobs if the factory closed.

She knows that her father has worked hard all his life for the business. He is a kind man at heart and he cares about the town and its people. She knows that the factory makes pills to reduce the pain of rheumatism.

But she also knows that her father has failed to clean up the water because it would cost too much. She knows the problems the pollution has caused.

Here are two extracts from Claire's diary:

MAY

Monday 11th

Another argument is going on. I'm in my bedroom but I can't help hearing. Mum's on at Dad again. They are talking about the purification plant. Dad says he can't afford it. I think she's right...

MAY

Tuesday 12th

Today Dad had a letter from an old lady. She told him how much his drug had helped her rheumatism. Suddenly I can't help seeing things differently...

Activity

- Now finish this diary entry.
  Include all the reasons why Claire thinks her mother is right.

Activity

- Now finish this diary entry.
  Include all the reasons why Claire now thinks her father could be right.

Solution

THE DEMONSTRATION BEFORE THE GATE CONTINUES.

WHAT CAN WE DO?

THERE IS A NEW VISITOR.

HOW DO YOU DO. MY NAME IS ENRICO SUAREZ AND I WORK FOR THE SECTION OF THE EUROPEAN COMMISSION THAT DEALS WITH POLLUTION AND THE ENVIRONMENT.

GULP.. SO I'M GOING TO BE FINED BY THE E.C. AS WELL?

NOT IF YOU AGREE TO SOLVE THE PROBLEM RIGHT AWAY. YOU MIGHT GET AN E.C. GRANT FOR THE PURIFICATION PLANT YOU NEED.

THAT'S GREAT! HOW DO I GO ABOUT APPLYING?

I CAN HELP YOU WITH THAT

What would you do?

Chris, Raheela and other characters in the story are faced
with many difficult decisions. They are not alone!
Life is full of difficult decisions.

Activity

- Six situations are described on the following pages. In each one a difficult decision must be made.
- In groups, read about each situation in turn and discuss:
  - What you **could** do
  - What you **should** do
  - What you **would** do

CAN IT BE RIGHT TO STEAL?

John Brown's wife is suffering from cancer. John hears about a wonderful new drug. It is made by a big drug company. It has taken the company twenty years to develop the drug, and cost them millions of pounds to make.

The price of the drug is £5000. John does not have the money. He borrows £2000 and offers it to the company. He says his wife will die if they do not help.

The company refuses. They say that if they sold the drug cheaply to Mr Brown, then other people would want the same. If they did not charge the full price they would lose money.

That night John breaks into the company's offices. He steals the new drug and gives it to his wife.

Was he right?

CAN YOU TAKE THE OFFER?

You are the Chairman of a Formula One car racing team. Your wife was a very heavy smoker. A year ago she died of lung cancer.

Your team has been sponsored by a soft drinks company. Last year your team lost many races, and the sponsor pulled out. The team is in a very difficult position. It was about to buy a new star driver. Now the team cannot afford him. At the last moment a new company offers to sponsor the team. But there is one problem. It is a tobacco company.

You are in two minds. Your team really needs the new deal. But your wife died from smoking. Do you accept the offer?

WOULD YOU GO ON TELEVISION?

You work for a company that sells burglar alarms. Many of your customers are old people. You know that many sales staff get old people to buy alarms by frightening them with stories of break-ins and muggings.

You are invited to appear on a programme which tells the truth about these sales. If you go on the programme and tell the truth, your friends at work will feel you are letting them down. You might also lose your job.

On the other hand, you feel that it is wrong to frighten old people into buying alarms. Do you agree to go on the programme?

DO YOU KEEP THE MONEY?

Your money has been taken by the school bully. Walking home you see something lying on the pavement. It is a wallet. Inside there is a pension book with a name and address on it. There is also £50.

You want to keep the money to buy a new computer game. At the same time, you recognise the name and address on the pension book. It is the grumpy old man who lives round the corner. Do you keep the money?

WOULD YOU TAKE THE COMPUTER AND RUN?

You go to a big store and buy a computer. You pay with a cheque. The assistant is very busy and makes a mistake. Instead of taking the cheque and giving you a receipt, he gives you your own cheque back and puts the receipt in the till.

Do you keep your cheque – or do you go back in and pay?

HOW CAN YOU HELP?

You go to a new school and are worried about being bullied. A tough girl called Kelly becomes your friend and looks after you.

Then another new girl called Sharon arrives in the class. Kelly starts to bully Sharon. Sharon comes to ask your advice. Should she report Kelly for bullying? You hate to see Sharon being bullied. But Kelly is your best friend because she looked after you when you were new. What advice do you give Sharon?

How am I doing?

Review your own progress as speaker and listener.

Make notes first. Then discuss them with two or three other people.

Seek and offer advice.

As a speaker

How am I different from the way I was two years ago?

When do I talk easily and well?

What holds me back?

What might help?

As a listener

When have I really listened?

What is it that gets me listening?

What prevents me from listening?

What might help?

As a member of a group

Which group situations bring out the best in me?

How would other people describe my group work?

Do I always behave in the same way in groups?

When doesn't it work? What might help?

Drama

What have I learned from drama?

What kind of tasks do I respond to well?

When doesn't it work?

What might help?

Contributing to groups

In a group, discuss these four situations.

- What are the other people thinking?
- Can you suggest three good tips to improve each situation?

Situation 1

Situation 2

Situation 3

Situation 4

HELP

Running groups

Roles in the group are:

- Chair   • Scribe   • Spokesperson   • Note taker   • Timekeeper

In Year 9, you should be able to take on all of these roles.

There are other kinds of role too:

- The person who has ideas
- The person who asks sensible questions
- The person who brings you back to the job in hand
- The person who is always thinking things through
- The person who always looks at it from another point of view

What other roles can you think of?

Which ones do you take?

All the roles are good roles. You need to be able to take them all.

Activity

Set yourself two personal targets for speaking and listening this term.

Choose something you need to improve. Keep it simple.

For example:

- I will speak in every group discussion
- I'll offer to chair a group, and be spokesperson in another group
- I won't butt in
- I will show more interest in what other people say by asking questions
- I will join a group with different people
- I'll put my hand up at least once every lesson
- I will take notes to help me listen for longer

UNIT SIX

What the Dickens!

In this unit, you will read passages by one of England's most famous novelists, Charles Dickens.

Dickens spent much of his life in London but it was very different from the London we know today. It was overcrowded and noisy. Once, almost forty people were found to be living in a single room! There was disease. Many children died when they were very young. The city was full of thieves and prostitutes, and people lived in dreadful poverty. Criminals were treated harshly by the law. Prisons were terrible and Londoners still flocked to see public hangings.

However, London was a lively, bustling and colourful place with its markets and street entertainers.

Each evening, Dickens used to walk up to ten miles through the streets of London to get ideas for his writing.

Dickens' London

In this passage from *Great Expectations*, Pip, the main character in the novel, has just arrived in London. He goes for a walk.

So, I came into <u>Smithfield</u>; and the shameful place, being all asmear with filth and fat and blood and foam, seemed to stick to me. So, I rubbed it off with all possible speed by turning into a street where I saw the great black dome of St Paul's bulging at me from behind a grim stone building which a <u>bystander</u> said was Newgate Prison. Following the wall of the jail, I found the roadway covered with straw to deaden the noise of passing vehicles; and from this, and from the quantity of people standing about, smelling strongly of spirits and beer, I <u>inferred</u> that the trials were on.

Activity

- List four things about London which Pip finds unpleasant.

- Write a short description of a town or city you know well. This time try to make it sound attractive.

  Here are some ways in which you could do this:

  Describe pleasant sights, sounds and smells

  Describe friendly people

  Describe attractive buildings

  Describe pleasant weather

★ Glossary

Smithfield = the famous meat market

bystander = passer-by

inferred = guessed

Dickens captures the reader's attention

Read the opening of *Great Expectations*. Pip, a small boy, is
alone in a graveyard. He becomes afraid and begins to cry.

 'Hold your noise!' cried a terrible voice, as a man started up
from among the graves at the side of the church porch.
'Keep still, you little devil, or I'll cut your throat!'

   A fearful man, all in coarse grey, with a great iron on his leg. A
man with no hat, and with broken shoes, and with an old rag tied
round his head. A man who had been soaked in water, and
smothered in mud, and lamed by stones, and cut by flints, and
stung by nettles, and torn by briars; who limped, and shivered,
and glared and growled; and whose teeth chattered in his head
as he seized me by the chin.

A good writer will try to capture the reader's attention at
the beginning of a novel in order to make them want to read on.
Often, the reader will want to know more and feel curious about
what might happen next.

Activity

- Write down five questions you would like to ask
  about this opening, for example:
  Who is the man in the graveyard?
- In pairs, discuss what you think might happen next.

HELP

Try questions which begin with the
words 'Who', 'What', 'When' and 'Where'.
Don't forget to use question marks.

The man is an escaped convict and he wants Pip to help him.

Activity

- List three things the convict might want Pip to do for him.

- Suggest two ways in which he might make Pip do as he says.

Pip lives with his horrible sister and her husband since both his parents are dead.

- With a partner, act out the conversation Pip might have with his sister when he gets home from his terrifying meeting with the convict. You will have to decide whether he tells her what has happened. Think about the following points:

How do you think Pip felt?

What will he say to his sister?

Should he tell the truth?

- Write a short script of your conversation. Set your work out like this:

Pip's sister: *Where have you been?*

Pip: *Out.*

Pip's sister: *Out where?*

Pen portraits

Dickens was one of the best-loved writers of his day. His imagination helped him to create **characters** for his stories which are so vivid, they seem almost real. Dickens spoke about his characters as if they were real, rather like you might discuss a character from a soap opera as if he or she were a real person.

Here are some of Dickens' most well-known and best-loved characters.

Smike

'an anxious and timid expression'

'patched and tattered'

'lame'

'dispirited and hopeless'

'could not have been less than eighteen or nineteen years old'

'round his neck was a tattered child's frill'

'timid, broken-spirited creature'

'shrunk back as if expecting a blow'

Fagin

'very old and shrivelled'

'villainous and repulsive face'

'matted red hair'

'dressed in a greasy flannel gown'

'bright dark eyes'

'a threatening attitude'

'rubbed his hands with a chuckle'

Estella

'very pretty and seemed very proud'

'beautiful and self-possessed'

'as scornful of me as if she had been one-and-twenty, and a queen'

'I found her irresistible'

'indescribable charm'

'her pretty brown hair spread out in her two hands'

'She laughed contemptuously'

Mrs Squeers

'a large raw-boned figure'

'dressed in a ... night-jacket'

'with her hair in papers'

'a dirty night-cap ... yellow cotton handkerchief which tied it under her chin'

'presiding over an immense basin of brimstone and treacle'

Activity

• Here are two more pen portraits. Use Dickens' words and your own ideas to sketch them.

The Artful Dodger

'one of the queerest-looking boys that Oliver had ever seen'

'snub-nosed'

'flat-browed'

'dirty'

'all the airs and manners of a man'

'bow-legs'

'little, sharp, ugly eyes'

'as ... swaggering a young gentleman as ever stood four feet six'

Uriah Heep

'a red-haired person'

'a youth of fifteen ... but looking much older'

'hardly any eyebrows, and no eyelashes'

'high-shouldered and bony'

'dressed in decent black'

'buttoned up to the throat'

'long, lank, skeleton hand'

Naming names

Dickens enjoyed creating names for his characters.

Activity

- Here are some of the names of characters in his novels. Read them to a partner.

Mr Bumble	Mr Boffin
Mr M'Choakumchild	Tiny Tim
Mr Squeers	Mr Gradgrind
Mr Guppy	Mr Murdstone
Mr Pickwick	Betsey Trotwood
Mr Podsnap	Mr Pecksniff

- Choose the three names you like best. For each one:

1. Discuss what the character might look like

2. Decide how the character might behave

3. Draw a picture of the character

4. Write a short description of your drawing of the character like those on pages 111–113

Dickens paints a picture

In *Great Expectations*, a young boy called Pip goes to visit an old lady called Miss Havisham. Pip has not met Miss Havisham before. He arrives at her house feeling rather nervous. This is what he sees...

 In an armchair, with an elbow resting on the table, and her head leaning on that hand, sat the strangest lady I have ever seen, or shall ever see.

She was dressed in rich materials – satins, and lace, and silks – all of white. Her shoes were white. She had a long white veil and bridal flowers in her hair, but her hair was white. Some bright jewels sparkled on her neck and on her hands, and some other jewels lay sparkling on the table. Dresses, less splendid than the dress she wore, and half-packed trunks, were scattered about. She had not quite finished dressing, for she had but one shoe on – the other was on the table near her hand – her veil was but half arranged, her watch and chain were not put on, and some lace for her bosom lay with those <u>trinkets</u>, and with her handkerchief, and gloves, and some flowers, and a prayer-book, all heaped about the <u>looking-glass</u>.

I saw that everything within my view which ought to be white, had been white long ago, and had lost its <u>lustre</u>, and was faded and yellow. I saw that the bride within the bridal dress had withered like the dress, and like the flowers, and had no brightness left but the brightness of her sunken eyes. I saw that the dress had been put upon the rounded figure of a young woman, and that the figure upon which it now hung loose, had shrunk to skin and bone.

> ★ **Glossary**
>
> **trinkets** = small items of jewellery
>
> **looking-glass** = mirror
>
> **lustre** = shine

Activity

- Write down five things you have learned about the lady. For example:

  She is wearing only one shoe.

- Draw a picture of the lady, including all the details in the passage such as:

  – Her white hair   – Her wedding dress   – Her veil

  – Her jewellery   – The flowers in her hair

  If you like, you could trace over the outline below and add the details.

The lady is Miss Havisham. She is an old lady. Why do you think she is dressed like a bride? Pip visits Miss Havisham again. On this visit, he is taken into another room. This is what he sees:

The daylight was completely <u>excluded</u>, and it had an airless smell. Smoke hung in the room, colder than the clearer air – like our own marsh mist. Certain wintry branches of candles on the high chimney-piece faintly lighted the chamber. It was <u>spacious</u>, and I dare say had once been handsome, but everything in it was covered with dust and mould, and dropping to pieces. The most <u>prominent</u> object was a long table with a tablecloth spread on it, as if a feast had been in preparation when the house and the clocks all stopped together. A centre-piece of some kind was in the middle of this cloth; it was heavily overhung with cobwebs and as I looked along the yellow expanse out of which I remember its seeming to grow like a black fungus, I saw speckled-legged spiders with blotchy bodies running home to it, and running out from it.

I heard the mice too, rattling behind the panels. The black-beetles took no notice and groped about the <u>hearth</u> in a <u>ponderous</u> elderly way, as if they were short-sighted and hard of hearing, and not on terms with one another. These crawling things had fascinated my attention and I was watching them from a distance, when Miss Havisham laid a hand upon my shoulder. In her other hand she had a crutch-headed stick on which she leaned, and she looked like the Witch of the place.

'This,' said she, pointing to the long table with her stick, 'is where I will be laid when I am dead. They shall come and look at me here.'
With some vague <u>misgiving</u> that she might get upon the table then and there and die at once, I shrank under her touch.

'What do you think that is?' she asked me, again pointing with her stick; 'that, where those cobwebs are?'

'I can't guess what it is, ma'am.'

'It's a great cake. A bride-cake. Mine!'

★ **Glossary**

excluded = shut out   **hearth** = fireplace

spacious = large   **ponderous** = heavy

prominent = obvious   **misgiving** = fear

Activity

- Make a list of six things you can find in the picture below, which are described in the passage. Use the exact words from the passage, like this:

speckled-legged spiders with blotchy bodies

When Miss Havisham was a young woman, she was going to be married.
The man she was going to marry jilted her. This means that he decided not to marry her just before the wedding.
This broke her heart and she never recovered. Everything in the room has been left just as it was all those years ago.

Dickens has painted very clear pictures of Miss Havisham and the room. One way in which he has helped us to imagine the scene is by using **adjectives**.

An adjective is a word which describes something, for example:

bright jewels

young woman

blotchy bodies

long table

Activity

Look through either the description of Miss Havisham on page 115 or the description of the room on page 117. Find ten adjectives which describe things clearly.

- Describe three people. In each case, use one significant detail that really gives a sudden, sharp impression.

- Write a long paragraph describing a person or a place.

- Share your description with a partner. Pick out the three best words or details used.

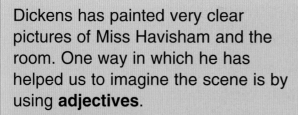

HELP

Descriptive detail

Clever writers use one or two important details instead of a full explanation. The details give you a sudden, sharp impression.

A good example is the way many writers describe a person's face by telling you about just one feature, for example:

He had cruel eyes.
Her mouth was a red gash.
She had plump strawberry lips.

Writers also choose surprising adjectives, for example:

Blotchy bodies
Speckle-legged spiders

Dickens only tells us one thing about Miss Havisham's face: the brightness of her sunken eyes.

Goosebumps

Pip is frightened by what he has seen at Miss Havisham's house. Later, in the garden, he thinks he sees something:

It was in this place, and at this moment, that a strange thing happened. I thought it a strange thing then, and I thought it a stranger thing long afterwards. I turned my eyes – a little dimmed by looking up at the frosty light – towards a great wooden beam in a low <u>nook</u> of the building near me on my right hand, and I saw a figure hanging there by the neck. A figure all in yellow white, with but one shoe to the feet; and it hung so, that I could see that the faded <u>trimmings</u> of the dress were like earthy paper, and that the face was Miss Havisham's, with a movement going over the whole <u>countenance</u> as if she were trying to call me. In the terror of seeing the figure, and in the terror of being certain that it had not been there a moment before, I at first ran from it, and then ran towards it. And my terror was greatest of all, when I found no figure there.

★ **Glossary**

nook = corner

trimmings = decoration

countenance = face

Activity
- What did Pip see?
- Find two details which make the vision especially horrible.
- Find words that are repeated to emphasise how scary it was.

A Christmas Carol is another story by Dickens. In *A Christmas Carol*, Ebenezer Scrooge is a miser. He hates spending money and he doesn't like people to enjoy themselves. One Christmas, he is visited by four ghosts. The ghosts teach Scrooge that he should be more kind and more generous. Read these descriptions of three of the ghosts:

It was a strange figure – like a child; yet not so like a child as like an old man. Its hair, which hung about its head and down its back, was white, as if with age; and yet the face had not a wrinkle in it, and the tenderest <u>bloom</u> was on the skin. The arms were very long and muscular; the hands the same, as if its hold were of uncommon strength. Its legs and feet, most delicately formed, were bare. It wore a tunic of the purest white; and round its waist was bound a <u>lustrous</u> belt, the <u>sheen</u> of which was beautiful. It held a branch of fresh green holly in its hand; and had its dress <u>trimmed</u> with summer flowers. But the strangest thing about it was, that from the crown of its head there sprang a bright clear jet of light.

It was clothed in one simple deep green robe bordered with white fur. This garment hung so loosely on the figure, that its breast was bare. Its feet, beneath the folds of the garment, were also bare; and on its head it wore no other covering than a holly wreath, set here and there with shining icicles. Its dark-brown curls were long and free; free as its <u>genial</u> face, its sparkling eye, its open hand, its cheery voice and its joyful air. Round its middle was an antique <u>scabbard</u>; but no sword was in it, and the ancient sheath was eaten up with rust.

The Phantom slowly, gravely, silently approached. It was <u>shrouded</u> in a deep black garment, which <u>concealed</u> its head, its face, its form, and left nothing of it visible, save one outstretched hand. But for this, it would have been difficult to detach its figure from the night, and separate it from the darkness by which it was surrounded. The Spirit neither spoke nor moved.

★ Glossary

bloom = rosy pink colour

lustrous = shiny

sheen = brightness

trimmed = decorated

genial = friendly

scabbard = a case for the sword

shrouded = wrapped like a dead body

concealed = hidden

Activity

- Look at the illustrations of the three ghosts. Match the illustrations to the descriptions on page 121.

Activity

- Find three words or groups of words from each description on page 121 that helped you to match it to the illustration.
- Think about how the ghosts are described.
  1. Which is the most friendly? Give two reasons for your answer.
  2. Which ghost sounds the most strange? Give two reasons for your answer.
  3. Which ghost sounds the most frightening? Give two reasons for your answer.

Oliver Twist is a story Dickens wrote about cruelty to children.

In *Oliver Twist*, the **orphan** Oliver is sent to live in a **workhouse**.

★ Glossary

orphan = a child whose parents have died

workhouse = a place like a prison where poor people had to live. Conditions were usually very bad.

George Cruikshank

Activity

- Read the following passage. Oliver is made to ask the master for more food.
- Think about how Oliver felt and what the master might do.

The room in which the boys were fed was a large stone hall, with a <u>copper</u> at one end, out of which the master, dressed in an apron for the purpose, and assisted by one or two women, ladled the <u>gruel</u> at meal-times. The bowls never wanted washing. The boys polished them with their spoons till they shone again. Oliver Twist and his companions suffered the tortures of slow starvation for three months: at last they got so wild with hunger, that one boy, who was tall for his age, and hadn't been used to that sort of thing (for his father had kept a small cookshop), hinted darkly to his companions, that unless he had another basin of gruel, he was afraid he might some night happen to eat the boy who slept next him, who happened to be a weakly youth of tender age. He had a wild, hungry eye; and they believed him. A <u>council</u> was held; <u>lots were cast</u> who should walk up to the master after supper that evening, and ask for more; and it fell to Oliver Twist.

The evening arrived; the boys took their places. The master, in his cook's uniform, <u>stationed himself</u> at the copper; his pauper assistants ranged themselves behind him; the gruel was served out; and a long <u>grace</u> was said over the short commons. The gruel disappeared; the boys whispered each other, and winked at Oliver, while his next neighbours nudged him. Child as he was, he was desperate with hunger, and reckless with misery. He rose from the table, and advancing to the master, basin and spoon in hand, said: somewhat alarmed at his own temerity:

'Please, sir, I want some more.'

★ Glossary

copper = large pot

gruel = thin porridge

council = meeting

lots were cast = had a draw to decide something

stationed himself = stood

grace = prayer said before a meal

So what's new?

Dickens wrote *Oliver Twist* in 1837. Here are two more novelists talking about boys. One is writing nearly 80 years later, and the other is writing about 150 years later.

From 1913:

William remained a year at his new post in Nottingham. He was studying hard, and growing serious. Something seemed to be fretting him. Still he went out to the dances and the river parties. He came home very late at night, and sat yet longer studying. His mother implored him to take more care, to do one thing or another.

'Dance if you want to dance, my son; but don't think you can work in an office and then amuse yourself, and then study on top of it all. You can't; the human frame won't stand it. Do one thing or the other – amuse yourself or learn Latin; but don't try to do both.'

From *Sons and Lovers* by D.H. Lawrence

From 1992:

Simon Martin sprawled over the three chairs outside the staffroom door. He'd been sent there for being a nuisance in Assembly. He'd only arrived four minutes earlier, and already he was bored halfway out of his skull. He'd tried whistling (and been told off for it by Miss Arnott on her way in). He'd even tried seeing how many different clicking noises he could make with his tongue (and been told off for it by Mr Spencer as he walked past).

From *Flour Babies* by Anne Fine

Compare the passages from *Oliver Twist*, *Sons and Lovers* and *Flour Babies*, and explain what changes you can see over time.

 HELP

Comparisons

Look for changes in:

- The content, e.g. behaviour, lifestyle
- The language and style, e.g. vocabulary, expression
- The tone or approach, e.g. how formal it is, the voice of the narrator

It helps to organise your thoughts if you make a grid with the three features down the left-hand side, and the names of the novels across the top.

Activity

Read the passage from *Oliver Twist* again.

- Find five things that are typical of Dickens' writing.
- Describe Dickens' style of writing.
- How does Dickens make you sympathise with Oliver?

HELP

Perspective

Perspective is viewpoint. It's where we stand as we follow the events of the story. For example, Dickens makes us see the events through Oliver's eyes. He does this by:

- Telling us how Oliver is feeling
- Telling us what Oliver is thinking
- Telling us what Oliver sees and does
- Describing Oliver's suffering
- Not telling us much about the other characters
- Using words which influence our reactions, e.g. 'reckless with misery'

Activity

- What do you think might happen to Oliver as a result of him asking for more?

  Choose one of the following:

  1. He is given some more food
  2. He is beaten
  3. He is thrown out of the workhouse
  4. He gets a telling off

- In pairs, act out the scene four times trying these different reactions.

- Write a short passage (about 12 to 15 lines) which continues the story of Oliver after he has asked for more.

HELP

Writing in the style of Dickens

- Read aloud the passage from *Oliver Twist* to get the feel of the language.

- Borrow one of his long sentences and use your own words in it.

- Think like a Victorian, write 'in role'.

- Use the same kind of grand words.

- Borrow some of the words Dickens uses.

- Keep up the big, confident voice of someone telling a story.

- Include several descriptive details instead of 'big picture' statements.

Although Dickens wrote about very serious things he wrote about them in an amusing way. His writing would make people laugh.

Activity

- Now read what happens next in the story of *Oliver Twist.*

> The master was a fat, healthy man; but he turned very pale.
> He gazed in stupefied astonishment on the small rebel for
> some seconds, and then clung for support to the copper.
> The assistants were paralysed with wonder; the boys with fear.
> 'What?' said the master at length, in a faint voice.
> 'Please, sir,' replied Oliver, 'I want some more.'

- Write down three amusing things about the way the master and his assistants are described.

A grisly end

Not all of Dickens' writing is humorous though. Later on in the story *Oliver Twist*, Oliver joins a gang of pickpockets. Among the people he meets is a burglar called Bill Sikes, and Bill's girlfriend Nancy. Nancy knows that Bill is bad and she goes behind his back to help Oliver. Bill finds out. Nancy begs for mercy, but he murders her.

The <u>housebreaker</u> freed one arm, and grasped his pistol. In the midst of his fury he beat it twice with all the force he could <u>summon</u>, upon the upturned face that almost touched his own.

She staggered and fell, nearly blinded with the blood that rained down from a deep gash in her forehead; but raising herself, with difficulty, on her knees, drew from her bosom a white handkerchief, and holding it up in her folded hands, as high towards Heaven as her feeble strength would allow, breathed one prayer for mercy to her <u>Maker</u>.

It was a ghastly figure to look upon. The murderer staggering backward to the wall, and shutting out the sight with his hand, seized a heavy club and struck her down.

What reaction does Dickens want from the reader?

How does he get it?

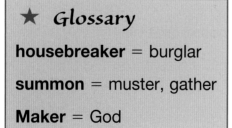

★ *Glossary*

housebreaker = burglar

summon = muster, gather

Maker = God

Bill Sikes from a cartoon of the time

Dickens used to give public readings of his novels. He even toured America. The death of Nancy was a favourite reading and members of the audience wept and fainted to hear of her murder.

CHARLES DICKENS'S

DRAMATIC READINGS

AS READ IN AMERICA.

DOCTOR MARIGOLD.

BOSTON:
LEE & SHEPARD, Publishers.
1876.

Towards the end of *Oliver Twist*, Bill Sikes goes on the run. He is chased. He falls from a rooftop as he tries to escape. Read the last passage on page 130 to find out what happens.

Roused into new strength and energy, he set his foot against the stack of chimneys, fastened one end of the rope tightly and firmly round it, and with the other made a strong running <u>noose</u> by the aid of his hands and teeth almost in a second. He could let himself down by the cord to within a less distance of the ground than his own height, and had his knife ready in his hand to cut it then and drop.

Staggering as if struck by lightning, he lost his balance and tumbled. The noose was on his neck. It ran up with his weight, tight as a <u>bowstring</u>, and swift as the arrow it speeds. He fell for five-and-thirty feet. There was a sudden jerk, a terrific <u>convulsion</u> of the limbs; and there he hung, with the open knife clenched in his stiffening hand.

> ★ **Glossary**
>
> **noose** =
> a loop of rope
>
> **bowstring** =
> a cord on an
> archer's bow
>
> **convulsion** =
> a jerking
> movement

Activity

- Imagine that you are a reporter. The murder of Nancy and the death of Bill Sikes would make a great news story.

- Work with a partner. Your partner should take the part of a witness to Nancy's murder.

- Interview your partner.

- Now swap roles. Your partner is the reporter. This time you are a witness to the death of Bill Sikes.

- Act out this interview with your partner.

Dickens' life and times

Activity

• Look at the timeline of Dickens' life below. The coloured text shows historical events that occurred at the time.

• Why do you think he wanted life for poor people to be better?

1812	Dickens born
1815	Napoleon beaten by English at Battle of Waterloo
1823	Dickens lived in prison because his father was deep in debt
1824	Began work aged eleven in a bottle factory
1833	Slavery abolished in England
1835	Became a reporter at the House of Commons
1836	Married
	'Chartists' start their campaign to improve life for poor people
1837	Queen Victoria crowned
1838	Wrote *Oliver Twist*
1840s	These were called the Hungry Forties because life was so bad for poor people
1840	Laws passed to stop child labour
1842	Went to America to speak out against black slavery
1843	Wrote *A Christmas Carol*
1848	Political riots all over Europe
1850	Started a magazine to publish novels in monthly instalments
1858	Started giving public readings of his work
	Left his wife (they had ten children)
1861	Wrote *Great Expectations*
	Start of the American Civil War
1870	Education for all
	Dickens died. Buried in Poets' Corner at Westminster Abbey

Dickens and society

Dickens lived during the 1800s. In his novels he wrote about things which he felt were wrong with society such as:

- poverty
- slums
- cruelty to children
- dangerous working conditions
- crime
- bad schools
- the legal system.

In many of his novels he wrote about the poor, the weak and the lonely people in society. He hoped that conditions for real people like them might improve.

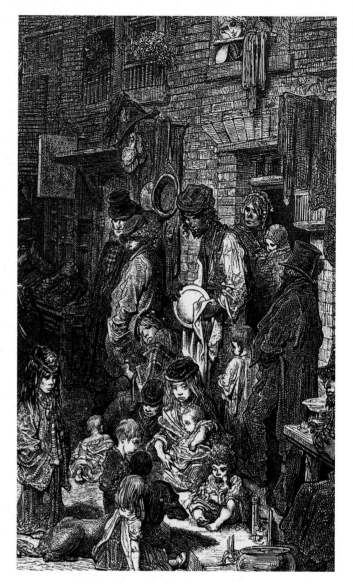

Activity

- Imagine yourself 1,000 years in the future. You are writing a story about the terrible life endured by teenagers like yourself in the early 21st century. Write any twenty lines from your novel. Use some of Dickens' techniques.

Usage Activities

The Usage section consists of exercises to help those pupils who may need to focus more attention on sentence structure and use of punctuation. Teachers may find it helpful to use the unpunctuated extracts, which are generally linked to the units through subject content, as a basis for whole-class or group-led discussions on the effect punctuation has on meaning and comprehension.

Usage – Unit One
Using reference and quotation

When writing about a book, referring to parts of the book can help to explain the point you are making. Sometimes it is more appropriate to use quotations. The following examples show the difference between referring and quoting.

Example 1: referring

Lord Lancaster is portrayed as a typical villain in his treatment of his young sisters and his nightly visits to the jail.

Example 2: quoting

Lord Lancaster is portrayed as a typical villain who is 'cunning and cruel', 'vile in his demeanour', with strange compulsions that take him 'lurking among the cells of the prison' and make him a 'torment' to his young sister.

HELP

Quote if:

- The quotation is pithy and apt.
- There's something significant in the wording.
- You are providing evidence about the language.
- It says it better than you can.
- You can find a way to fit the quotation into your own sentence.

Refer if:

- It's too long to quote.
- It's easy to put into your own words.
- The actual words used aren't significant.

Activity

- Use the following quotations about the setting of a story to practise writing sentences that integrate quotations:

  'a dry and desolate canyon'

  'baked hard in the heat of the sun'

  'rock and heat'

  'the sun hammered the sandstone rocks until they glowed red like blood'

  'a deathly hush gripped the canyon'

  'all was dead and silent'

  'bleached bones'

  'even vultures scorned this lonely place'

- Identify three things you can say about the way the setting is described.
- Find relevant quotations to use in each sentence.
- Fit the quotations neatly into the grammar of the sentence.

Punctuation

Read this extract taken from a novel set in the last century, about a man on the run in an American desert. He has just sensed danger.

> He limped half crouched down a ridge top to some boulders and squatted behind them tightening the bloody bandana on his thigh groaning quietly from the pain. Then he pulled the crossbow off his back his hands moving over the coffee-coloured wood with familiarity bred over a lifetime. It had been his grandfather's. Swanson knew the hearth stories – the old man had used it to poach deer and boar off the great English estates around Kent in the late 1700s. It must have been a wonderfully efficient weapon for the purpose powerful accurate silent as soft wind through spring leaves.

Five commas and a colon are missing from the extract. Write out the extract putting in the missing punctuation.

Spelling and vocabulary

Activity

Here are ten words that have the same '-ful' ending as 'powerful':

grateful	peaceful
faithful	dreadful
wonderful	thoughtful
spiteful	pitiful
beautiful	careful

- What spelling rule applies to words ending in 'e' or a consonant before the suffix. What rule applies to words ending in 'y'?
- Give the meaning of each of the following words as used in the extract:

  familiarity

  efficient

  accurate

Usage – Unit Two
Shaping paragraphs

> **HELP**
>
> When you are composing a paragraph you need to consider the following points:
>
> - Collect similar points together.
>
> - Run them into one sentence if it can be done without losing detail or meaning.
>
> - Look for complex rather than compound sentences (use a variety of connectives rather than 'and' or 'but').
>
> - Explain rather than list facts.
>
> - Put similar points next to each other.

Read and consider how the following points have been composed into a paragraph on the topic of packing clothes for a walking trip:

- comfortable
- easy to wash, non-iron
- light to carry
- warm
- jumper, thick socks, vest, T-shirts, underwear
- sponge bag
- plasters, antiseptic cream, wipes
- good shoes – thick soles, worn in
- backpack – comfortable shoulder straps, big, light, rainproof

Pack clothes that will be warm and comfortable, washable and light to carry. It may be cool and rainy, so choose a warm jumper, thick socks, and a waterproof coat with a hood. Underneath, you'll need vests, T-shirts and two changes of underwear. Most of all, you'll need a good pair of thick-soled walking shoes, already worn in. Don't forget your sponge bag and something for the blisters such as wipes, antiseptic cream and plasters. Put them in a large, light, rainproof backpack with comfortable shoulder straps. Even in the worst weather, you will be comfortable and well protected.

Activity

- Use the following points to compose a paragraph arguing the case for making First Aid a compulsory subject in schools:
  - Obviously useful, saves lives
  - Useful for careers in healthcare, sport, childcare
  - Could fit within an existing subject, e.g. PE, or be an option
  - More useful than some other subjects
- Aim to write four sentences. Try to choose an engaging introductory sentence. Link the points so it doesn't sound like a list, and draw a conclusion.

Punctuation

You may perhaps be part of a big family. Read the extract from *How Not to Raise the Perfect Child* by Libby Purves and see if you agree that life can be unfair.

In the days of big families[ ] children grew up knowing from an early age that life is unfair[ ] it was clear to the merest toddler that some people are bigger than others[ ] get their clothes brand new instead of handed down[ ] and are allowed penknives[ ] in a family of four or more children[ ] the laws of probability dictate that at least one other child seems to have had a better birthday than you[ ] and that someone else is[ ] in turn[ ] furiously jealous of yours[ ] it is noticeable in later life that the sons and daughters of big families make friends easily[ ] but also that they eat much faster than only children[ ] this is because they spent their formative years desperate to get the second helpings before the food ran out[ ]

Write out the extract putting in the missing punctuation. Afterwards, discuss what triggers the use of a comma, and why full stops are different.

Spelling and vocabulary

HELP

'Families' is the plural of 'family'. If words end with a consonant + 'y', change the 'y' to 'ie' before adding 's'.

Activity

Here are eight more words that follow that spelling rule:

donkey	battery
monkey	baby
boy	factory
play	alloy

- Write each word in its plural form.
- Use each word in a sentence.
- Give the meaning of each of the following words as used in the extract:

  dictate

  jealous

  formative

Usage – Unit Three
Describing literary effects

When writing about texts, we have to provide evidence for our claims. If we have an impression, we need to explain where we got it from and what techniques the writer has used to create it.

> **HELP**
>
> Consider the following bullet points before writing about literary effects.
>
> - Trust your own responses.
> - Pick up the mood and impression as well as the facts.
> - Start the sentence in a way that will oblige you to answer the question.
> - Mention two or three impressions, not just the first obvious thing.
> - Find relevant quotations.
> - Pick out the best quotations and summarise the others.
> - Round off by explaining how the writer achieved the effect.

Read the following extract carefully.

> Swanson eased over the crest of the trail. The pain was bad in his leg. He lay still for a long time in a patch of dried hopsage and listened to the hills. No sound. The morning sun burned into him. He squinted his eyes and searched for movement. The wind had died. Just heat dust and gravel. The flies and gnats hadn't started in yet. The air felt pure and clean and hot. He crawled forward until he was overlooking a wide canyon that fell sharply away from where he lay concealed. At the bottom he could see a rocky flat and dry river bed; a line of stunted tamarisk trees, parched and almost lifeless, bordered the waterless course of the river. Nothing looked alive.

What are your impressions of the place and the man?

Activity
- Referring to the Help Box, write a paragraph explaining how the writer creates an impression of intense heat.

Punctuation

Unit Three gives you the opportunity to enjoy *Macbeth*, a play written by William Shakespeare. However, history has a very different view of Macbeth and his wife. Read the following extract carefully.

Eleventh-century scotland was a violent and troubled country... macbeth was born into this violent world in 1005[ ] son of the great family that ruled moray and ross[ ] his own father was murdered by his cousin[ ] macbeth married gruach[ ] granddaughter to a high king of Scotland[ ] they had no children of their own[ ] there is no historical evidence about lady macbeth's influence on her husband[ ] duncan's rule had been ineffectual and unpopular[ ] he was thirty-eight when he was killed[ ] possibly by macbeth[ ] who was elected high king of Scotland in 1040[ ] macbeth ruled for seventeen years[ ] for the first ten as a competent[ ] reforming king[ ] he gave Scotland a long period of comparative peace and stability[ ] there is no evidence that macbeth dabbled in witch craft[ ] indeed[ ] he was a strong supporter of the church[ ]

Write out the extract as two paragraphs putting in all the missing punctuation. Don't forget that proper nouns need capital letters.

Spelling and vocabulary

Activity

The word 'unpopular' has the prefix 'un'. Here are ten words that have the same prefix:

unconventional	unofficial
unemployed	unpleasant
uncommon	unsatisfactory
unnecessary	unpredictable
unperfumed	unreadable

- What does 'un' mean?
- Why is there a double 'n' in 'unnecessary'?

- Use each word in a sentence, for example,

  The strong wind made our walk a very unpleasant experience.
- What other prefixes have the same meaning? For example, irreplaceable.
- When would you use each of them? Is there a rule?
- Give the meaning of each of the following words as used in the extract:

influence	competent
ineffectual	supporter

Usage – Unit Four
Drawing conclusions

What are the qualities you normally associate with the last paragraph of a piece of writing? Endings do vary. A writer may want to:

- Give a feeling of conclusion or closure, a satisfying ending
- Round up key issues
- Restate main points
- Pass a clear judgement
- Point to the future

Read the following two concluding paragraphs:

From a review of school pens

So there it is: the fountain pen is your best-value choice of writing tool. It is neat, reliable and only a little more expensive than its main competitor, the biro. Opt for tradition!

From a letter of complaint

As you will realise, the day was an expensive disappointment and left us with no alternative but to leave within an hour of arriving. As a result of these experiences, I wish to claim a refund of our entry fee amounting to £56. I look forward to receiving a cheque from you.

Are any of these features shown in the conclusions?

- A judgement
- A general summary
- A snappy or attention-grabbing phrase at the end

Activity

- Write the concluding paragraph of a review of a computer game that has made these points:
  - Aimed at eight- to fourteen-year-olds, but really only suitable for younger users
  - Cheap
  - Graphics are colourful and amusing
  - Repetitive, not very challenging
  - Helpline proved useful
  - Similar to other well-known games
  - End of game is spectacular
  - See back of handbook for useful 'cheats'.

Punctuation

Unit Four helps you to prepare for the Checkpoint tests.

Activity

Worst ever writing (only try this once)**!**

- Use the points below to help you write a passage that will remind you of the things you need to avoid when taking the test.
  - Forget to put in paragraph breaks
  - Make obvious spelling mistakes
  - Put commas instead of full stops
  - Write in a flat, unvaried way
  - Provide evidence but don't explain it
  - Do anything else that you personally need to remember you should not do
- Write your passage in blue or black and then highlight all your deliberate mistakes in colour.
- Share your passage with a partner. Does your discussion increase the amount of colour?

Spelling and vocabulary

Paper 2 of the test focuses your attention on the impressions you gain from your reading and the way the writer uses language to create impressions.

Activity

The words and phrases in the chart are very useful when describing literary effects.

- Find **two** alternative words or phrases with similar meaning to each word or phrase in the chart. One has been done for you. Use the list under the table to help you.

creates an impression	
suggest	
builds up	
create	
appeals to	
captures	secures
mood	
symbolises	

represents, evoke, engages, escalates, imply, suggests, stands for, paint, portray, conjures up, gathers, attracts, atmosphere, arouses, sense

Usage – Unit Five
Verbs and tense change

Read the following extract from a teacher's account of life in a Mongolian village as the middle of winter approaches.

> I wake up and my world has frozen. Everything, and I mean everything – my water, tomato paste, soap – is encased in thick, milky ice. I light a candle, stand up in my sleeping bag and pull on another layer of clothing. Shivering, I take a knife to the water bucket and hack at the ice until bubbles rise to the surface. Lighting my small stove is tough because the wood, which was damp, is now frozen.

Activity
- Write out the passage and underline or highlight all the verbs.
- Rewrite the passage in the past tense.

Punctuation

Here is a continuation of the extract about life in a Mongolian village, but the punctuation is missing. Read it carefully and then write it as three short paragraphs adding the missing punctuation. You will need to use full stops, commas, speech marks, a question mark and an exclamation mark.

> on this dark freezing winter morning venturing to the communal outside toilet is an endurance test but after two cups of coffee I am bundled up and off to work just as the sky is gradually brightening my school is a ten minute walk alongside the hovd river which flows through the village the river is now so frozen that the horses are being ridden and cars driven over it everything but my eyes is concealed from the freezing air – even my gloved fingers are pushed deep down into my pockets Louisa – off to work calls my neighbour sansa-hu don't worry he teases me its warm today – just wait till it gets really cold

Spelling and vocabulary

Activity

Here are ten words that can be used as verbs:

prepare	radiate
receive	predict
protest	recognise
rhyme	proceed
provide	recommend

- Check their meaning and learn how to spell them.
- Use each word in a sentence with the ending 'ing' or 'ed', for example, I prepared the meal myself.
- Give the meaning of each of the following words as used in the extract:

venturing

communal

gradually

concealed

Usage – Unit Six
Informal and formal 2

Read the following informal 'first person' account of an accident.

I was driving home on the M25. It was quite late, and the rain was bucketing down. I was only doing 50 because I couldn't see far enough ahead to be doing any more. The first I saw of the white van was at the end of the slip road at junction 10, as he was zooming along, charging onto the motorway. He must have been doing well over 70, more like 100. He only had one light on, so it was hard to tell where he was exactly. He just veered straight out in front of me, so I had to brake. I managed to slow down, but not enough to stop before I clipped his rear wing and we both swerved onto the hard shoulder. I got out of the car and saw the other driver topple out of his door.

Activity

- Write a report of the accident for an insurance claim. Remember to write in the 'third person'. Pick out the main details from the personal comments. Start your report:

  The accident occurred at Junction 10 of the M25 motorway.

Punctuation

HELP

Apostrophes can be used to show possession – the owner of something.

An 's' is usually added to the apostrophe unless the word already ends in an 's'.

Home belonging to a boy – the boy's home

Home belonging to two or more boys – the boys' home

Skills that one doctor has – the doctor's skills

Skills that belong to several doctors – the doctors' skills

Usage activities

In Unit Six you were introduced to the stories that Charles Dickens wrote. He tried to show some of the difficulties boys like Oliver Twist had to deal with in their lives. Oliver was an orphan. He had no family. However, sometimes being part of a family can be difficult. The boys in the following extract are trying to deal with the problem of living with their father, Andy.

> The boys lived with their father in andys home town of dukinfield[ ] and the girls lived with their mother in ashton[ ] the girls home was small[ ] tidy and comfortable[ ] but the boys had to get used to andys untidy ways[ ] the house was cluttered with his papers[ ] books and thousands of electronic parts and half-finished machines and kit which he was always intending to mend[ ] but never did[ ] it was a paradise of toys[ ] instruments and gadgetry[ ] a childs world rather than a mans[ ]
>
> The boys lives were turned upside down as they tried to fit in with their fathers lifestyle[ ] but they always felt that something was incomplete[ ] after a month[ ] they felt like strangers in their own lives[ ] and after several weeks[ ] they stopped trying to try[ ] their home was simply different from the girls[ ] messier but easier[ ] and that was when they accepted it[ ] and relaxed[ ]

Write out the extract putting in the missing punctuation. There are eight apostrophes of possession (see Help Box on page 145), plus full stops, commas and a colon. Don't forget capital letters at the beginning of sentences and for proper nouns.

Spelling and vocabulary

Activity

Here is a list of ten of the most commonly misspelt words:

atmosphere	knowledge
conscience	explanation
environment	listening
engagement	miscellaneous
industrial	chocolate

- Check their meaning. Use each word in a sentence.
- Learn how to spell them by finding words in each of them, for example,

  atmosphere – at, sphere, he, here

  knowledge – know, now, no, owl, ledge, edge.

Usage answers

Unit One – Punctuation

He limped half crouched down a ridge top to some boulders and squatted behind them, tightening the bloody bandana on his thigh, groaning quietly from the pain. Then he pulled the crossbow off his back, his hands moving over the coffee-coloured wood with familiarity bred over a lifetime. It had been his grandfather's. Swanson knew the hearth stories – the old man had used it to poach deer and boar off the great English estates around Kent in the late 1700s. It must have been a wonderfully efficient weapon for the purpose: powerful, accurate, silent as soft wind through spring leaves.

Unit Two – Punctuation

In the days of big families[,] children grew up knowing from an early age that life is unfair[.] It was clear to the merest toddler that some people are bigger than others[,] get their clothes brand new instead of handed down[,] and are allowed penknives[.] In a family of four or more children[,] the laws of probability dictate that at least one other child seems to have had a better birthday than you[,] and that someone else is[,] in turn[,] furiously jealous of yours[.] It is noticeable in later life that the sons and daughters of big families make friends easily[,] but also that they eat much faster than only children[:] this is because they spent their formative years desperate to get the second helpings before the food ran out[.]

Unit Three – Punctuation

Eleventh-century Scotland was a violent and troubled country... Macbeth was born into this violent world in 1005[,] son of the great family that ruled Moray and Ross[.] His own father was murdered by his cousin[.] Macbeth married Gruach[,] granddaughter to a high king of Scotland[.] They had no children of their own[.] There is no historical evidence about Lady Macbeth's influence on her husband[.]

Duncan's rule had been ineffectual and unpopular[.] He was thirty-eight when he was killed[,] possibly by Macbeth[,] who was elected high king of Scotland in 1040[.] Macbeth ruled for seventeen years[,] for the first ten as a competent[,] reforming king[.] He gave Scotland a long period of comparative peace and stability[.] There is no evidence that Macbeth dabbled in witch craft[,] indeed[,] he was a strong supporter of the Church[.]

Unit Four – Spelling and vocabulary

creates an impression	conjures up, suggests
suggest	evoke, imply
builds up	escalates, arouses
create	paint, portray
appeals to	engages, attracts
captures	secures, gathers
mood	atmosphere, sense
symbolises	represents, stands for

Unit Five – Punctuation

On this dark, freezing, winter morning, venturing to the communal outside toilet is an endurance test, but after two cups of coffee I am bundled up and off to work just as the sky is gradually brightening.

My school is a ten minute walk alongside the Hovd river, which flows through the village. The river is now so frozen that the horses are being ridden and cars driven over it. Everything but my eyes is concealed from the freezing air – even my gloved fingers are pushed deep down into my pockets.

'Louisa – off to work?' calls my neighbour Sansa-hu. 'Don't worry,' he teases me. 'It's warm today – just wait till it gets really cold!'

Unit Six – Punctuation

The boys lived with their father in Andy's home town of Dukinfield[,] and the girls lived with their mother in Ashton[.] The girls' home was small[,] tidy and comfortable[,] but the boys had to get used to Andy's untidy ways[.] The house was cluttered with his papers[,] books and thousands of electronic parts and half-finished machines and kit which he was always intending to mend[,] but never did[.] It was a paradise of toys[,] instruments and gadgetry[:] a child's world rather than a man's[.]

The boys' lives were turned upside down as they tried to fit in with their father's lifestyle[,] but they always felt that something was incomplete[.] After a month[,] they felt like strangers in their own lives[,] and after several weeks[,] they stopped trying to try[.] Their home was simply different from the girls'[,] messier but easier[,] and that was when they accepted it[,] and relaxed[.]